Dedication

I want to dedicate this project of mine to my wonderful and loving wife Gretchen, my treasured kids Zach & Margo, my daughter-in-law Amanda and my family and great friends. You all never gave up on me and I always appreciated your visits and words of encouragement.

And to my best friend Pastor Dave who helped nurture my faith and listened to my calls for spiritual help. I also want to mention Pastor Kevin who is the leader of our little Bible study group. Many of the postings I have had on Facebook needed a better mind than I could bring into the fold and Kevin was always there to advise me of a better way to deliver the message I attempted to convey. I love you all.

To the reader

The gate to the narrow road opens:

I don't remember what happened. I know Gretchen and I
were at the bar/restaurant with friends after the Snow
Queen event that night in which Margo was giving up the
crown she had earned the year before and we were going
out for a short time. That was 14 November, 2009. The first
memory I had that I could recall was on the Tuesday before
Thanksgiving that year, a day I believed to be the 26th of
November.

I was flown to Fargo and was comatose for a time. The
brain injury was and still is the injury that bothered me the
most. One of the vertebra that was fractured was the C-1,
the main target a hangman looks for to complete his job. It
was close.

Forward

I remember getting the phone call, "David's been in an accident." It sounded so innocent at the time, as a pastor I have gotten similar phone calls many times before. As a firefighter and fire chaplain I had run many accidents over the years. This time it was different, I heard the concern in Gretchen's voice as she said, "He's been flown to Fargo." Gretchen was being so strong but as she continued telling me what was going on I knew that this wasn't an ordinary accident, this was bad, and this was my best friend, over a thousand miles away.

Over the next days we waited and we prayed, over the next weeks we prayed and we waited and through it all, God worked miracles. The fact David is still alive is a miracle, the fact he has recovered like he has is the result of his tenacity and the incredible power of prayer. This is a book of hope, of promise, of God's love.

Who would have known over 20 years ago, a quick invitation to serve on my internship committee would result in a friendship that has stood the test of time, distance, job changes, kids growing up, and all of the things life throws at us.

2 men, 2 David's, 2 sports fans, 2 men of faith – we don't rank up with King David when it comes to chasing God's own heart – but we are men who are knit together with God's love and mercy. This is the story of my best friend, his recovery, his journey, his faith, and God's Amazing Grace.

God Bless you, DC – and thank you for allowing us to glimpse God's hand in your life. ~ Pastor Dave Brobston

Something to think about...

November 19, 2009 at 10:28am

Written on Facebook by Margo Christenson

What happened to my family has made me realize how important it is to be thankful for what you have in life. Take the time to show the people you care about how much they mean to you because you don't really know what is going to happen and who is going to be there tomorrow. Appreciate all of the little things in life that you take for granted: your ability to talk, to move, to remember, to see, to be able to breathe on your own, to eat whatever you want. These may seem like silly things to appreciate, but those abilities can go away in the blink of an eye.

I know it's hard at times, but don't hold grudges and be mad about the little things that happen. You don't know which words will be your last words to someone, so really try to make all of them kind. Appreciate what you have and the friends and family in your life so that you know if something were to happen, you showed them you cared and they knew how much you loved them.

Cherish the moments that you share with the people you love. The past few days I have realized how many little things I shared with my dad that I never appreciated. I miss the random text messages he would send me throughout the day that I knew he was just sending as an excuse to talk to me. Dad, whenever you are better and can read this, you can text me whenever you want, even if there is nothing you need to tell me. I miss randomly visiting my dad in his office that he was so proud of and raiding his cupboards for Oreos, mints, and candy. I didn't realize how much I truly enjoyed sitting there with my dad, listening to him rant about politics and tell me a bunch of random facts and sports scores from years ago that nobody should be able to remember. I never realized how much I took having my dad's constant support for granted. He probably missed 3 track meets from my 7th grade to senior year, and you can bet that he expected updates and times from not only my races but everyone else's too. Every other time, I could count on seeing my dad standing at the finish line with a stopwatch around his neck, telling me good job and ready to give me times and splits from all of my races. He even came to all of my concerts, even though I told him he didn't have to and I knew they were boring for him. I know on Sunday I will be waiting for my dad to text me parts of the Vikings fight song or SKOL VIKINGS! after every big play or Viking touchdown.

For all the kids that are reading this, I know sometimes it's hard to put your family in front of your friends, but please take some time to be with them. My dad asked me last weekend if I wanted to watch the state football games on TV with him but instead I wanted to go out and be with my friends. Now I wish I would have spent that extra time with him because I know how much it would have meant to him. We don't realize how much the smallest things to us, like sitting down and eating dinner or watching a movie with our mom and dad means to them. Take some time out of your day to actually have a conversation with them and maybe even hang out with them every now and then. It would mean the world to them.

For all of the college kids reading this, please take a few minutes out of your day to call or even just text your parents. I know sometimes it's hard because you are busy with friends or homework, but your parents think about you constantly while you are gone. For everything they have done for you, they deserve a few minutes of your time. Check in with them, tell them what is going on in your life, in school, what you did for the day, anything. You have no idea how much they appreciate that.

It is in times like the kind my family is in right now where you realize how important family and good friends really are. Thank you to everyone who has been praying for my dad and my family because we would not be so strong if we weren't surrounded by so many loving people. We are overwhelmed with all of the prayers and support that we have gotten over the past few days and we are thankful to have so many people by our side, waiting just as we are for my dad to make a full recovery. I am waiting for the day that I come home and see my dad sitting on the couch watching football or the history channel with his laptop in front of him and a bowl of popcorn beside him. I am waiting for the day when I can go visit my dad in his office again and sit there and really listen to everything he has to say. I have always been my "daddy's girl" and I can't wait until I can give him a "Margo-hug" again. I know I have so much more to learn from my dad, and I am praying each day that the time where he will be himself again comes soon.

1

The Edge of the Abyss
December 12, 2009 at 8:35pm

The road back has been hard but it will get harder and more difficult so it will be up to me to get all the way back along with the help from my dear and close family.

My story of my journey from the edge of the abyss really started about the 14th of November. Prior to that day I was a relatively healthy American male. Married for just over 25 years to Gretchen who teaches math at Britton-Hecla High School in Britton, SD and with two wonderful college age kids. Zach is a chemical engineering major at School of Mines in Rapid City, SD and Margo who is a Mass Communications major at St. Cloud St in St. Cloud, MN.

Earlier that day, I was out to our pasture and helped sort our calves from the cows for the purpose of weaning the calves from their mothers. Then around noon I went to my family's farm to drive semi truck for my Dad and brothers like I have for a few years now. I made sure to mention to my brothers that I needed to leave the farm by about 6:00 that evening so could get back to town to shower and get ready to attend the Snow Queen pageant to watch Margo give away the crown she had earned the year before.

This is where my journey really got complicated. After the pageant which I understand was wonderful, some of us and our friends decided to go out for supper and a cocktail or two. Somewhere after the supper and a Coor's Light or two I started feeling the effects of being working since before the sun rose that morning and told Gretchen I was going to walk home for the night. This was a walk of about 15-16 minutes and one that I had done many times before.

About 5 minutes out the door and just a handful of blocks from where I started I was struck by a car and run down. The driver took off and has yet to be found. I am sure the driver is not a local person and was probably in town for just the weekend anyway.

I was left lying in the street near the railroad tracks and was reported to the local cops and the local EMT squad. My clothes were all cut off me as taking them off would only have risked further injury. The EMT squad and one of the cops thought that I had head injuries (true) and possible spine injuries (also true).

I was shipped off to the local hospital for further treatment while my family was being notified. My wife was first to know as she had gotten home and I wasn't there but a notice from the hospital was. She then called Margo who was out with friends while on the way to the clinic. My family got to the cliinc and watched much of the proceedings.

I was not conscious and was air lifted to Merit Care in Fargo, ND. Ironically 10 years earlier I was flown to Merit Care for a heart problem. When I got to Fargo the physicians there started taking care of business while my family was driving the 120 miles in the dark to get here. I was totally out of contact with the world and would be for over a week. I was eventually diagnosed with 7 fractured neck vertebra, a fractured scapula, 2 broken ribs and a broken right leg damaged just below the knee along with a brain injury.

I'm not even sure exactly how long I was out of the loop but while under I knew I had been hurt but didn't know how or who had been hurt with me. I had no memory of the night it happened and still do not. All I can say is that I was very happy to wake up and see my great family around me and that I was able to communicate with everyone.

I am home now and will have many appointments headed my way these next 2 months. I am able to walk with the aid of a walker and I will eventually regain what I lost in mobility and in how I think and remember. My wife has taken on a new second job as my personal nurse these past few days and is doing a wonderful job keeping me going and on my toes.

There is more to this story that I am not ready to write yet but maybe soon I can do so.

2

40 days....
December 23, 2009 at 4:49pm

Soon it will be 40 days since my accident. I think about how things were before the accident and how they are today. I do not have the ability and the flexibility these days to do those "little" chores of those long ago days. I will someday get those abilities back but it will be a ways away and I will need to invest time and effort to achieve this feat.

Everyone wants to know how I'm doing and what I'm doing and my thoughts about the way things are now. So this is "The Rest of the Story."

My days now consist of waking up before Gretchen needs to get ready for school. Then Gretchen will clean and flush my chest tube for the day and also check the dressings on my right ear. I mostly am able to dress myself, a feat some days considering the stupid socks I need to wear to limit blood clots. Most days Gretchen will then help me with my physical therapy before I finally grab my walker and move my way to the dining room table for some breakfast cereal and the ever present meds.

I then make my way to the couch and click on FOX News and fire up my computer so I can get caught up on my Mob Wars, Mafia Wars and the events of my friends this day. Then around the mid part of the morning somebody, Gretchen or Zach and Margo, take me to my occupational and speech therapies at our local hospital here in Britton. These usually take me about an hour and a half to complete before I can catch a ride back home for a noon dinner prepared by either someone in my family or a family friend who has volunteered for duty.

Since the accident had made me quite tired these days I take a nap for awhile after I get done with dinner. After the refreshing nap I make my way back to the living room and turn the TV back on and also grab my computer. Sometimes I also will get a book to read. My attention span isn't what it used to be so the reading has suffered a bit here of late.

I watch movies, sports or news and weather while reading what is going on in the cyber world on the computer while waiting for Gretchen to return from school. I wait until supper is prepared and when that is done I once again return to the couch/TV/computer to wait until it is time for my shower and bed time. I am really kind of liking the showers because then afterwards I get to lay perfectly still while looking directly at the ceiling and Gretchen can then remove my neck collar and replace the abrasive "pads" that are fitted on the side of the collar that is closest to my skin. I have taken to growing a pathetic beard these days with the collar after all the nurses and doctors at Merit Care in Fargo said that by doing so I will likely experience less whisker, facial and neck irritation from the "pads".

This life style is really starting to grate on me but I have no real choices at this time until I finally can get well enough to return to driving and work which will hopefully start the last week in January; about 2 1/2 months after the accident.

Some of the things that I read about and look at while embedded behind my computer are about hit and run accidents (11% of all accidents are hit and run) and the Aspen collar (a very high percentage of those who can't use the Aspen get fitted with a Halo or they are paralyzed) I wear. I also am fortunate enough where I get some visitors from time to time.

I have been very humbled by this ordeal. I have seen people give time and efforts to helping me and my family time and time again. Many of these people are those I wasn't even aware knew of our existence. We are also getting cards, notices and gifts in the mail everyday from friends, relatives and also those people who we never have known except in name only. I am ever grateful of all of this and I trust and hope that this awful experience I am having is one that I learn from and that nobody has to also live through. I will be much more diligent in other's unfortunate incidences and do my best to help them in their time of need.

3

Almost missed Christmas....

December 25, 2009 at 6:48pm

For the first time ever I almost missed Christmas this year. It wasn't by design to say the least. It was by accident or should I say "by an accident.'

If there are any who care to read this and they don't know the story, I was struck by a hit and run driver on the night of 14 November. I was air lifted to Merit Care in Fargo and things were touch and go to say the least. My mind is still not back to where it was but it is getting better.

I was able to go out to Mom and Dad's house yesterday to partake in the usual Christmas Eve there. It was so much fun to have supper with all of my family and I very much enjoyed the conversation. We were actually able to laugh at some of the things I said and did while in the hospital in Fargo. Like when I motioned to both Roger and Scott to some closer to me just after the therapist left my bedside and I then told my brothers I expected them to bust me outta there and that I was also expecting them to get me home where I could then rest on my own couch. Then there was the time when I told Dad that "they" had done this to me about 3 years ago and "they" still couldn't get me. The first time "they" had left me in the bull rushes and I had gotten away. It seemed that all that were there to hear that story knew then that I probably played Mob Wars on Facebook too much or involved myself in too many video games and movies. But all in all it was a joyous time last night with the family.

With the blizzard today no travels were in order so the Tishers stayed home and Gretchen, Margo, Zach and I had our own Christmas Day dinner. After a short nap by me we took part in a good game of Farming, something we hadn't done in eons. It was so fun to play this game with those I hold most dear to me. Having a day with Gretchen, Zach and Margo was simply an awesome moment for me.

Hopefully many of these stories remain just in our memories of 2009 and none of the worst things repeat themselves and the good stuff does and maybe even multiplies like playing games with each other on a cold and snow packed day that no travel is advised.

4

Another mulligan.....
January 3, 2010 at 5:06pm

I don't golf much anymore but when I did my good friends were always ready to give this hacker a mulligan when the ball wouldn't go where it should have gone. They had seen me swing a club before and the results weren't always very cool to watch so being the kind souls they were they would offer me a mulligan to take another shot at the fairway.

My life has taken a few variances over the 50+ years of existence. The ones I can remember and care to relay in this note are the time I got run over by the farm loader tractor and broke my pelvis when I was about 4 1/2. I had to spend 6 weeks in the hospital and then another 6 weeks at home. All of this time was spent in bed. I had to learn how to walk again and was walking with a very noticeable limp when I first started school. I'm guessing that this all made my Mom a nervous wreck many times over.

Then there was the mini-bike incident where I was giving my youngest brother a ride and flipped the bike. Both of us went flying but we were both lucky in that Scott walked away unscathed and I broke both bones in my left arm. 12 weeks with the arm in a cast for a 12 year old in summer must have been tough for my Mom.

Also coming to mind in my formative days was when I was driving my brother Roger and a friend of his and also my sister Janet to the girls basketball tournament in Sisseton. We had gotten some snow some days prior and after the sun and wind took their turns the road was an enigma as there were clear dry spots and icy areas that were unseen in the darkness. I went to pass a car and when I kicked open my 400 4-barrel Oldsmobile the back end of the car passed the front and we were going about 60 some miles an hour backwards down the road. We ended up spinning around a few times and the back of the car finally came to a stop just short of the farmer's fence on the other side of the right hand ditch about 30 feet from the road. Nobody was hurt except my pride. I think it was sometime before we told Mom of this one.

Now I am getting a bit more recent. On the 19th of March of 1999 I was air lifted to Merit Care in Fargo for what was called a myocardial infarction; a heart attack. I was implanted with 3 cardiac stents. Incidentally this hospital was destined to receive me via helicopter at least once more in the future. I weathered this mulligan as well as a 39-year old could by doing my best at trying to become an airplane pilot but that was not to be as when I went to renew my medical license I failed the stress test and had to have another stent implanted and the FAA refused to renew the medical even though my cardiologist and also the flight surgeon in Aberdeen wrote letters to them stating their opinions to my good heart health. Oh well....Must have been too many mulligans for this round.... By this time I'm sure Mom just shook her head....

Now I am to the 14th of November of 2009. That was the fateful night I was run down by a hit and run driver. I had some extreme injuries that I will not recount here as I have already talked enough about them the past few weeks. In analyzing all the information and looking at the videos from the accident I was in I am convinced that I more than likely should not have survived. The car was estimated to be traveling 30-35 mph when it smoked me.

This is where my story really starts. I survived the heart attack scare by what I called the 3 "Fs".....family, friends and Faith....and not necessarily in that order. I am writing this today because of those same 3 "Fs" and I am giving most of the credit to my Faith. I am not naive enough to say that my Faith is stellar or complete. Just that it is strong enough so that when things are over and above what I can control there is a Higher Being that I can rely on.

I had some brain damage in the accident and I totally

cannot remember anything from that night, even events a few hours before the accident are gone from my head. I was care lifted to Merit Care, the north campus which is where the trauma cases pretty much go I guess. When I finally came to be aware of my surroundings I still had very little memory. Those of my friends and relatives that came to visit me are lost to the black zone that was my mind. I guess I recognized everyone and even knew their names but the recognition was fleeting. I started remembering events somewhere around Thanksgiving and can recall some of these things today but the most vivid memory I have at the north campus is almost surreal. The memory is seemingly quite real to me and I am the only person in it. I am in a narrow but long room on a narrow bed not unlike a gurney. I am watching this event from behind the head of the person on the gurney and the room is lighted by white lights and there is a plethora of yellow also in the room of which most of the yellow is around the bed. I realize that I am the one watching this going on but I am also the one who is on the bed. I am watching from behind and just below the top of the bed and all I can see of myself on the bed is the top of my head. I was moved to the south campus for rehab as I progressed in health but this dream has remained with me for me to try to contemplate.

I have thought many times about that dream and it has slowly come to me that maybe this was one more mulligan for me. My time on this earth was extended by my Maker maybe because I have enough faith to warrant it and also maybe so I can try to help one more person and that they won't need any mulligans in their life.

My favorite Bible verse is in Ecclesiastes 3. I believe that there is a time for everything and my time in this life obviously isn't done. I have felt for a long time that we humans all have a purpose in life and it is up to us to find that purpose and interpret it when it comes upon us.

I have tried to be upbeat by my injuries and this has been something I have been asked about. My firm reply is that even though I am not happy at being beat up and needing care from many others I recognize that this is something that will not last all that long in the scheme of things and that if I wanted to be upset and complain about these afflictions to anyone and everyone then I become a person nobody wants to be around or someone who seems to want everyone to feel sorry for me. If I can change the way one person's attitude about their problems and change it to the positive side, then I feel that maybe one of my life's purposes can be accounted for.

I have nurtured this faith as a life member and baptized member of First Lutheran Church here in Britton. I had my faith confirmed by pastor Don Gaarder in 1975. My great friend, pastor Dave Brobston helped me realize the importance of faith as I have grown older. These two pastors have helped me survive these mulligans in my life and I am grateful that they have given of their time to teach me and that they had enough faith in me to continue to hold true to their own Faith in God to help me understand what is more important in our lives on Earth.

My faith may not be as good as others or as unshakable as some of those around me but it is certain and absolute. There will always be room for improvement and God has granted me some more time to work on this so I won't need a mulligan in the future.

Matthew 11:28
Come to me, all of you who are weary and carry heavy burdens, and I will give you rest.

Ecclesiastes 3:1
For everything there is a season, a time for every activity under heaven.

5

Progress is in the wind....
January 7, 2010 at 9:39pm

We all know that here in NE South Dakota that winter is in full force. Lots of snow and plenty of wind have combined to make travel difficult at times and also has led to school cancellations.

But what I want to believe in is that there is progress in these South Dakota winter winds. I was released from Occupational Therapy care today as I am no longer deemed "of need" by them anymore.

I will find out tomorrow about Speech Therapy and if I am done there or will require a few more sessions. Personally, I would prefer a few more of these as it seems these sessions have been helping plenty the past couple of weeks. I still have some distance to go to get back to where I think I was prior to the accident but I also know I am getting closer to being there.

I started Physical Therapy with Amy Jo Vietor this past

Monday and that has gone fairly well. Not much for pain as far as I am concerned but I am getting upset with all the "snaps, crackles and pops" that I feel on every single attempt at almost every exercise. I am getting to the point where I am thinking that there is going to be significant damage to the ligaments in the right knee and also am thinking that along with the broken scapula that the rotator cuff and the muscles surrounding it and attached to the rotator cuff are also trashed and are going to be needing attention at sometime in the near future. An appointment with Dr. Miller in Aberdeen is scheduled for the 28th of January.

But first things first. I need to continue to work on these things and also I need to do the exercises to my neck as per Dr. Sieg's instructions. The neck is getting a bit more fluid in moving and this has been a good feeling mentally for me. I also know that it is still in a delicate state and will try hard to keep it's condition in my best interest. I am due to go back to Dr. Sieg in Fargo on February 9th.

I am thinking that 2010 has been cold and snowy but not all that bad for me in the scheme of things if I consider these issues. I will be able to at least start doing some work here at home in the next couple of weeks. I will still be unable to drive or go to my office until about February 1st. I can't wait for that moment....

6

A new step tonight... and etc....
January 16, 2010 at 3:37pm

My wife and I have something "new" to do tonight. I think that for the first time since the accident that we will both go out together somewhere at night. I have gone a couple of times to my investment club but I don't think both of us have gone somewhere at the same time.

We will be picked up at our house by some of our great friends and the 4 of us will go just a few blocks away to more friends for supper and conversation. Should be an awesome time for us but especially for me as it is one more step in trying to get back to "normal" in my life.

In other "news" since my last posted note I had a long day on Thursday. Roger drove me to Fargo for a neuropsychology test. Even Roger wasn't immune I guess as he was handed a test sheet to complete as I went into the closed door session. In my opinion there was a plethora of idiotic questions for me to answer. Most of the day was spent doing different things that ranged from spelling words, definitions of other words and hand and eye coordination tests. But about every hour or so I was handed a sheet of questions to fill out. These were multiple choice and the choices ranged from 1-5 with 1 being worst and 5 as best or the test was N for "never" and VT for "very true" with 3 other choices in between. These tests ranged from a low of 20 questions to about 40 until the very last one which was 352 questions. The idiotic part of this testing was that somewhere between 15-20% of these questions had to do with suicide, close to 15% was about drug abuse, a few less about alcohol abuse, and about 8% to 5% about violence and sex, in that order. I asked the lady why so many psychology type questions. She was quick to respond that it was not psychology but neuropsychology. I also had a HUGE problem with her early in the process when I was doing the definition stage. She would give words, words that we would use or words that would describe something that we do most every day, and I was supposed to give a definition of the said word. On one of these, I can't even remember which one it was, I gave a definition (it was a word that most of us will use almost every day) and the lady said she wanted "More" of a definition. I might have gotten just a bit irate at this point (I think we were 10-15 minutes into the whole testing process....) and I asked her what exactly she required of me with this test as the definition I had given to the target word was such that both she and I knew what it was and furthermore if we went out and asked anyone in the street about the said word that my definition was likely to be repeated. The testing lady just said that the words were scored by my definitions and she wanted me to get the highest score possible. I told her that was as high as I was going to get and that she should give me my points. Stupid tests.....

I have another appointment with the actual neuropsychologist and also my attending doctor from the south complex this coming Wednesday. The two of them will go over these test results at that time. Gretchen will be my driver that day and if all goes well I am hoping that I will be given clearance to be able to drive again soon and to actually go back to work too. I'm just hoping that the testing lady doesn't add that I was belligerent at her testing station....

Oh....and I must add at this time..... SKOL Vikings !!! Kick-off is at noon tomorrow against the dang Cowpokes at the Metrodome. I am leaving it up to everyone at the Dome, including my 2 brothers, to make this a miserable place for a cowboy to be.....

7

Winner's Creed
April 9, 2010 at 10:11am

One of the things I decided to focus on in the recovery process from my injuries sustained last November was to do my best to maintain as positive of an attitude that I could. I have used many tools to help in this process and one of these tools was the use of the internet. I found a "Winner's Creed" posted on one web site and I will post that in this note but not before I post a "Winner's Creed" that is one of the adornments hanging on the wall behind my desk at my office. I can't even remember when/where I got that message but I do remember that I had it mounted on the wall of my office for many years when I was selling John Deere machinery. So it has been in my possession for some time now.

~~~~~~~~~~

A Winners Creed

If you think you are beaten, you are,

If you think you dare not, then you won't.

If you like to win, but you think you can't,

it is almost certain you won't.

If you think you'll lose, you're lost.

For out of the world we find,

success begins with a fellow's will

it's all in the state of the mind.

If you think you are outclassed, you are

you've got to be sure of yourself before

you can ever win a prize.

Life's battles don't always go

to the stronger or faster man,

but sooner or later the man who wins

is the man who thinks he can.

(Author Unknown)

~~~~~~~~~

I found another "Winner's Creed" while surfing the 'net' a few weeks ago that I also like very much. I want to share it with my real life friends and my Facebook friends because I think it carries a message that is about the positives of Faith, of healing and the attitudes needed to succeed in our life's endeavors and celebrate the gifts that God has made available to those of us who Believe in Him.

~~~~~~~~~

Winner's Creed

I am a winner. I have faith in God. I believe in myself and I know that everything works for good in the end.

Whatever I do, whether I eat, drink, talk and walk, I will Win!

I am born to succeed and I will not allow anybody or anything to stop me from achieving success in life.

With God's help, I know I can do it because nothing is impossible with Him.

I will accept failure is a part of winning and I must learn to overcome defeat and emerge as a real winner.

I know I will win because I choose to begin, so help me God.

Amen.

(Unknown Author)

8

ZERO Hour approaches ....

November 14, 2010 at 8:23pm

As I start this writing it is 8:03 p.m. Central time. We are almost 2 hours from the exact time a year ago that I was run down by a hit and run driver. It has been an ordeal for the whole family and one that I am enjoying very much at this time because I realize even more now than before what Family, Friends and Faith really are. But it wasn't always a cheerful ride. I still need to get stronger, physically, mentally and spiritually. We are about 9 days away from shoulder surgery and as we have gone forward here of late, it seems as though that moment won't get here too soon.

In the past, my family laughed and joked about my ability to remember crazy and stupid like trivia. Like the scores of football games and baseball games from thirty-some years ago and places and names of other things and people that have crossed paths with me. I can still remember the combination, 20-30-6, from my 6th grade locker. I was able to remember phone numbers many times if I just dialed it up once or twice. Some of that is possibly over with because of the memory issues these days from that trauma.

But what concerns me today is that I can remember 'important' dates but not the MOST important dates. I can remember most birthdays and anniversaries. I can even remember the day I graduated from high school; May 18th, 1977 .... a Wednesday night. But I am at a total loss for remembering the day and date that I was baptized into my Christian faith. I know I was confirmed into my Lutheran faith in 1975, probably in May. I still have the leisure suit. LOL But I cannot remember that date either.

And I call those days and dates most important because it was in those days that my life was sealed into my Christian faith and strengthened me toward those traumatic events from one year ago. God granted me more time on earth and awarded me more patience in those trying days and nights. I have more work to do.

9

A Purpose

December 6, 2010 at 3:17pm

Just got back from Aberdeen where I had an appointment with Dr.
Miller who is my ortho doc and who also performed the SLAP tear
repair 2 weeks ago. Dr. Miller was very pleased at the progress of
the shoulder and the PT involved and even made the comment that I
"heal fast" to which I replied that I have always seemed to heal
fairly fast when I have been injured.

Before leaving the clinic Dr. Miller showed me the pictures of what
the shoulder looked like both before he performed the surgery and
after. And these pictures were showing the inside of the shoulder
and I was surprised that they were even in color. I was expecting
that if I was going to be able to see them that they would be infrared
and not in color. It was an amazing education as he took me through
the damaged areas and showed how he repaired them. An education
to say the least, but one that I kind of wish had not started the way it
did in November of 2009. As I went out to the lobby I signed
consent forms so that copies of these pictures could be sent to me. I
think they will be loaded to a diskette and therefore I can upload

them wherever I want so they might show up in my photos section here on Facebook.

While driving home I started contemplating that conversation with Dr. Miller and when I said that I have always seemed to heal fairly fast. Thinking this through even more I have come to the conclusion that God has always blessed me with the strength to heal when I have been hurt and then further blessed me with the faith and belief to trust in those who have the desire to help others, such as all the doctors, nurses and therapists I have been so fortunate to have had working with me these last 55 weeks.

Author and minister Rick Warren says in his book "Purpose Driven Life" that "Life is a series of problems: Either you are in one now, you're just coming out of one, or you're getting ready to go into another one. The reason for this is that God is more interested in your character than your comfort; God is more interested in making your life holy than He is in making your life happy." Well Pastor Warren, I can tell you that these are profound words. And I do feel that not only am I thinking I have a 'happy life' but that it is becoming more holy. But maybe it is likely that my life is becoming more holy and therefore is getting me happier as he says in his book. Probably doesn't matter as long as the holy thing solidifies itself each day.

When I was growing up back in the 60s and 70s here in South Dakota I had dreams of being the Minnesota Twins leftfielder. As I grew older and the curve ball became more of a nemesis for me I started the desire to become a Minnesota Viking instead. After all, it is easier to crash into another player than it is to hit a curve. No certain position, I just wanted to wear the Purple and Gold and have that cool helmet with the horns. And then to use this awesome uniform to deliver gut wrenching tackles on opposing ball carriers. All this time I think my Mom had aspirations of me becoming a minister as so many mothers desire for their sons to do along with being a doctor, lawyer or some other occupation like these. These things were not to be as I just was too short on talent for the sports world and wanted a more "exciting" profession than that of a minister. So I became the next best thing in my mind; I started farming and working the soil and watching my work grow and produce crops to sell. It was something to behold to watch God's workings in this way.

With God's blessing of me after those injuries from a year ago it kind of seems that maybe Mom had a vision of me being able to help others know the Word and to help spread His Word of Truth. I told my best friend, Pastor Dave Brobston, back in February that maybe my "accident" was a "purpose" and that it was a "purpose" for me to realize that I need to focus on my Faith. And that if this "accident" can bring "one more soul closer to God, then maybe it was a "purpose" that I can feel good about."

I also told Dave "I have learned from my accident....that my Faith in God is real. That Christ is the only real recovery in our human lives. That God gave His only Son to suffer so that I did not. That my faith in my family is well founded. That people take too many things for granted." I still have these text messages in my phone yet today.

As we near Christmas I ask that people will think of these kinds of messages and ask themselves if they are taking too much for granted. Ask yourself if you have told those you hold close to you that you love and care for them. Wonder if there is just one more thing you can do for others.

Ecc 3 says there is a time for everything. So the time has come for me to tell more of the "purpose" and I hope and pray that God has blessed me one more time with the strength to deliver a meaningful message to those who will read this note.

God bless everyone and have a very Merry Christmas. It is the season for the REASON.

DRC

10

Valentine's Day

Valentine's Day is almost over as I type this note. I haven't added much to my notes here of late that pertain to my recovery from those terrible traumas from 2009. But today is a day that just seemed to be one to do so.

I attended the memorial service this morning for Doug Smith. I was not one who some would think of as good friends with Doug. In fact, we really just started kind of hanging out some the past couple years. After all, he was a big Bears fan and I am a Vikings fan. Doug loved his Cubs too. The Twins are what interest me when it comes to major league baseball. But in the recovery process from last year my goal was to do my best to get to the physical level that would allow me to revisit Arizona for the spring training baseball games that my brothers, friends and I had seen the past couple years or so. I worked out quite diligently to get to that point and was able to do the AZ trip. We met up with Doug and his wife Vicky for that last day in sunny AZ to watch the Giants and Cubs play. Just a great day was had by all of us, but I didn't really recognize the meaning of it all until today. This was my first real time away from my dear wife and caretaker after those injuries almost stole that companionship away from us. I had wanted to get away and enjoy some baseball and a beer or two with my brothers and friends. I think Doug knew more than I did of how important it was for me to do this. You see, Vicky was also a victim of a vehicle/pedestrian incident many years ago before she and Doug met and Doug knew what Vicky had to deal with spiritually, mentally and physically when she was on her way back to better health and the ongoing afflictions in everyday life for years to come.

Doug just seemed to believe that this was going to happen for me and was possibly even happier than I was to be there with everyone. And to see me get out of the taxi at the ballpark and walk up to the two of them outside the stadium that day brought some hugs and handshakes to every one of us there that day. We all would likely say that this was a very special day for every one of us and one that we will cherish for a long, long time.

Doug's belief from that day made me think some more this afternoon of the enormity of that belief. In John 20:29 we are told 'Jesus said to him, "Have you believed because you have seen me? Blessed are those who have not seen and yet have believed."' In my self-reflection this afternoon it kept coming back to me that maybe Doug knew more of how I was going to be able to recover because he had the Faith and that he BELIEVED I could and would recover with God's help, more so than any of the rest of us might have had. Doug had not seen me for some time and was only getting reports from my brothers about how my progress was and what I was up to. Maybe even like the disciples got news of what Jesus was doing in days they weren't there to watch, listen and take part in His miracles and in His daily works. Yet Doug sure wasn't a Doubting Thomas. He just knew....he had a Faith that all of us Christians should do our best to attain in this life.

I will close this note with John 20:31:

But these are written so that you may continue to believe that Jesus is the Messiah, the Son of God, and that by believing in him you will have life by the power of his name.

Rest In Peace Doug my friend. I will remember you each time I put my Cubs cap on and what you have taught me in our short earthly time together.

11

The Maze

March 10, 2011 at 9:10am

I was asked recently where I was going and while I thought
it was obvious what the answer was at the time it still made
me think and ponder this question in more depth. I know
where I am going, just not exactly sure of the roads and
directions to get there all the time. The Maze is what I will
need to navigate in order to get to where I will finally end
in my earthly travels. I know that my destination is that I
will someday stand before God for my judgment. And His
verdict of my human life is the result of how I handled the
Maze and all its turns and puzzlements on this journey.

While I am not a fan of a maze I do have a strategy for
completing one. In my recovery process from the TBI my
therapy at different times was to do a maze. I was able to
remember my strategy and these types of mazes were
relatively simple compared to other daunting tasks assigned
to me from these therapists. I remember getting pictures of
different objects such as a broom, a haystack, a cow, sheep
and other things such as this and my task was to identify

the object by naming it. Many times I knew what it was and what it did but could not remember the name of the object. This was very, very frustrating to say the least. As far as the maze strategy, I would look at the starting point and then the ending point and trace the possible avenues back from there. Even though my brain damage was evident with the inability to recognize those objects I took less time than was expected to do a maze.

But in real life the Maze of our life is what God will use in His judgment of our time in His world. How we traverse through the many different life circumstances directed our way will determine His judgment of our very real final destination. I believe that in this Lenten season we need to remember and focus on this portion of our Maze.

Jesus wandered about in his desert maze for 40 days. Moses was in his maze for 40 years. We don't know how long it will take us to travel our own maze but we need to stop and ask Him for directions and guidance. Every part of that maze we travel could and should be used to connect with God. We also need to enjoy this travel through our maze. We need to laugh and have a good time. It is said in Proverbs 17:22 "A merry heart is a good medicine: but a broken spirit drieth up the bones."

I wish everyone a happy and safe journey through their Lenten and Easter maze.

DRC

For God so loved the world, that he gave his only Son, that whoever believes in him should not perish but have eternal life. ~ John 3:16

12

The Rooster Will Crow
April 17, 2011 at 2:39pm

Yesterday's First Lesson was from Isaiah 50. I almost smiled a bit when verse 6 says "I offered my back to those who beat me...." as it reminded me of my physical therapy that I am still doing two times a week for my shoulder. The part of the therapy that I speak of is some of the stretching when I lay down on my stomach and the PT brings my arm around to the middle of my back and cranks on it like a cop might do to a belligerent arrest suspect. Then in verse 6 "....I did not hide my face from mocking and spitting." This also brought a kind of smile to me as I have always thought of myself as a kind of macho tough guy and don't want others to know when I am hurt. But my PT knows I do hurt because I groan and have a labored breathing when under this duress. Isaiah 50:7-8 then says "Because the Sovereign Lord helps me, I will not be disgraced. Therefore I have set my face like flint, and I know I will not be put to shame. (8) He who vindicates me is near...." And I walk out of Torture Chamber #1 and all others greet me without the knowledge of the pain I just went through moments earlier. But I know better.....the Lord is with me. No doubt in my mind.

Jesus answered, "Will you lay down your life for me? Truly, truly, I say to you, the rooster will not crow till you have denied me three times. ~ John 13:38

This verse is starting to mean more for me today than it ever did before. It has made me think of my almost 52 years on God's earth and what I have done with those blessed 51+ years. Yes, I have faced many difficult and trying times. But I have always been able to rise up and go on without a lot of real issues. I have things that aren't easy to deal with but it could be worse, much worse. My shoulder is getting closer to being about as close to 100% of what it used to be from before I was struck down by that car in November 2009. My hip is better after the cortisone shot a couple weeks ago. The knee is weak and cracks a lot but not something that is overly tough to deal with as yet. I still have numbness in my face near the lower right side of my jaw. The worst is the constant ringing in my ears, loudest in my left. This is so much louder than most of my everyday sounds and is with me from the time I awake to the time I finally drift off to sleep each night.

Jesus told Peter these words after Peter told Him that he wanted to come with him and would lay down his life for Jesus. Peter was to fulfill this prophesy and realized it when he heard the rooster on Good Friday morning. In my lifetime, I was hurt when I was about 4 1/2 by the tractor when I was run over. I was flown to Fargo in 1999 for my heart attack and then again in November 2009 when I was struck down by that hit and run driver. I ask myself; Did I deny my Lord 3 times in these instances? In some ways I am starting to see what Peter might have felt when he heard that rooster crow.

For the most part I don't think I have really questioned my Faith. I know and admit it could be better and stronger. The biggest question I have given myself in this is whether I have denied Him and His word. I have faced 3 different and difficult circumstances that could have had such different outcomes. Why did God grant me more time? I have asked myself that question many times over the past 17 months. What am I to do? What am I supposed to do? My mind is filled with a plethora of these types of questions and yet I continue to fail to find the answers time after time.

It makes me think that maybe the answer, or at least a part of the answer, is to tell others of my life's maze and journey. I know and admit that I do not pray as much as He would like me to do. But I have a prayer that I use most every night when I go to bed. "Thank you God for giving me another day with those who love and care for me and with those I love and care for. Please bless me with the strength, wisdom and power to tell others of Your True Word and to help make a difference in Your world. Amen"

I hope and pray that everyone has a safe and Blessed Easter. I pray that I can make a difference in His world.

Let the same mind be in you that was in Christ Jesus, who, though he was in the form of God, did not regard equality with God as something to be exploited, but emptied himself, taking the form of a slave, being born in human likeness. And being found in human form, he humbled himself and became obedient to the point of death— even death on a cross
Therefore God also highly exalted him and gave him the name that is above every name, so that at the name of Jesus every knee should bend, in heaven and on earth and under the earth, and every tongue should confess that Jesus Christ is Lord, to the glory of God the Father. ~ **Philippians 2:6-11**

My quote of the day:
If God had wanted me otherwise, He would have created me otherwise. ~ Johann Wolfgang von Goethe

13

18 Months
May 14, 2011 at 11:03am

Tonight it will be 18 months since I was run down by that hit and run driver. Wow....it feels strange...... Sometimes it seems like it just happened. And then it seems like it was so long ago. But then I get to thinking that it was just a cruel nightmare that just won't ever end. But then reality sets in when my knee cracks, I get irritated at the ringing in my ears, I get frustrated at having to wear glasses again after having had such good results from the lasik surgery and being able to view the 20-15 chart without correction. Will it ever end?? I know some probably see me out and about and think I am "recovered" from those traumas. But the truth is, this will never happen. Some of that is because of the severity of those injuries and some the simple fact of my age at the time of the incident.

Nagging me some yet today is that somebody just left me to die along that street. They knew they hit a person. They hit their brakes twice, the evidence is there, but then just calmly drove away without a second thought to what their actions had accomplished, without caring what my family would go through regardless to whether I lived or not. So callous... So selfish... In my office I have police photos of the crime scene with me laying along the side of the street next to the railroad tracks. I have pictures of the possible car and the damage it sustained to the windshield. The owners have told investigators they "hit a pheasant at 65-70 mph" but can't explain the twin scratches on the hood that abruptly stop about midway from near the front of the hood to the smashed windshield. The investigators are still working the case but this is getting a bit harder for me to deal with. 18 months the perpetrator has lived with that knowledge without dealing with the consequences of their actions. It makes me wonder what is wrong with society these days. Have we gone our own way and away from our Lord and Savior? Um......probably considering that prayer is no longer allowed in schools, and that Christian life is viewed as something that many don't want in their own lives such as a Nativity scene on government grounds, maybe we have. Crazy I tell you, just plain crazy.

I know "how" I survived that terrible trauma. I just need to learn "why" I was able to. The "how" is because of what I have mentioned in earlier notes; The 3 F's ~ Family, Friends and Faith. And not necessarily in that order either. Family, because they give you strength. Friends, because they can give you hope. Faith, because it gives you all else. The "why" is still out there for me to find. Also addressed in earlier notes is my thought that maybe one of the reasons I was able to survive was that God has further plans for me. To help others learn of His True Word and that the only true recovery is in knowing that God gave His only Son to die for us on that cross so many years ago. He suffered on that cross so that we could have a chance to earn a place with Him after that final day of judgment. He suffered so that we would not have to. He endured pains that make ours so trivial. In watching Mel Gibson's "Passion Of Christ" on Easter weekend, a movie that Gretchen and I had seen when it was released some years ago, when Jesus was chained down and whipped I kept on thinking "Why do I think I was in such pain when He endured this with no second thoughts?" I wasn't very emotional before those traumas of 18 months ago but I do get there much easier now than before.

This is a pivotal time in the ongoing recovery of a TBI injury. With a TBI there are important dates of testing and the most telling are at 3 months and 18 months. Basically it sounds like whatever level of cognizance I am experiencing at the 18 month time frame will be my new normal, especially considering my age right now (51) and the age of trauma. These tests will most likely consist of strength and other physical tests, spelling, math, logic and the old standby stupid test: naming as many different animals/objects that start with a certain letter like "S" in one minute or less. Stupid tests I call them all.

At the start of this note I asked if my irritations, frustrations and other things about this will ever end. I know that they will end someday. When I stand before our God and Savior for my judgment of my life's journey through the Maze on God's earth, these things will end.

God, I thank you for giving one more day with those that love and care for me and those that I love and care for. I ask that You bless and grant me with the knowledge and wisdom, the power and strength to let others know of Your True Word and to make a difference in Your world. Amen.

"I shall tell you a great secret my friend. Do not wait for the last judgment, it takes place every day." --- Albert Camus

Behold, he cometh with clouds; and every eye shall see him, and they also which pierced him: and all kindreds of the earth shall wail because of him. Even so, Amen.
I am Alpha and Omega, the beginning and the ending, saith the Lord. ~ Revelation, 1. 7

14

Don't Miss The Dessert
May 21, 2011 at 11:01am

Gretchen and I went to a fund raiser the other night for the
purpose of helping with the cost of new bleachers at the
track and football field complex at Hugh Schilling Field
here in Britton. A great meal was served with a choice of
pork or beef sandwiches, beans, macaroni salad and two
choices of bars. When we were seated at a table with some
others a statement was made that I know I have either said
or at least thought to myself about it and I'm guessing
many others have also had the same thoughts. One of the
guys sitting at our table is named Al and he said that maybe
he should only have the dessert and bypass the rest of the
meal. We all laughed and this spurred further conversation
about that scenario and the types of desserts offered.

When I got home this popped into my thoughts again. It
made me think about desserts. We normally have desserts
at the end of the meal but some want it earlier or even in
that situation mentioned earlier, only the dessert. Most
everyone wants some. Sometimes we fill up on the meal

enough where we decide not to have any desserts. And most of us protect our choice of dessert with thoughts of not wanting to share it with anyone.

There are many different kinds and types of desserts making me think and compare dessert to religion. We have cookies, cakes, pudding, bars, pies, ice cream and others missing my list. Each one of these desserts also has different flavors. In religion we have Christians, Jews, Muslims, Hindus to name a few and many others. In turn, each religion then has different sects instructing on their idea of how to worship.

Some years ago I decided to get a Facebook account. After I made this account I mentioned this fact at supper one night and our daughter was very disappointed that I had done so. She said only "creepers" my age were on Facebook. I think she was a bit perturbed that maybe I was trying to spy on her, trying to keep tabs on what she was doing on Facebook. Part of the reason I did make this account was that one of the fantasy football leagues I had been in for quite a few years was talking of doing the league and scoring on Facebook and we all needed to create an account for this to work. The league decided not to do so and to satisfy our daughter's upset thoughts of me being on Facebook I deactivated the account.

Not very sure when I re-activated the account but I think it was almost 3 years ago. At that time I started playing Mob Wars which is a social gaming application that I really like playing. I have 'met' some really cool people through this venue over the past few years. Many of them paid close attention to my predicament when I was hurt in November, 2009. In exchanges of messages with these Facebook and Mob Wars people I have been able to better cope with the recovery work I have needed to do these past 18 months.

When I have become 'friends' with these Mob Wars players many times I go to their profile page to read up a bit on where they are from, what they like and look at whatever information is readily available for others to look at, the "creeper" in me I suppose. This past year and a half I have really paid attention to any religious views and comments. When I see that a person doesn't have any views, is apathetic or is just plainly a non-believer, I actually feel sorry for them and wish them God's blessings. Then I wonder if there would be anything I could do to help them know the true Word of God.

I feel that we all have chances to make a difference in our world and in God's world. We make decisions each day to this affect. Many things happen beyond our control too that upset the apple-cart and cause us problems with our best intentioned plans. God has granted each and every one of us the ability to make our own conclusions and decisions on how we deal with different things thrown our way. We can choose to make a positive difference or a negative difference. From the youngest person to the oldest person we all have had the ability to do this in one form or another.

I wonder if we desire to mostly fill up our time with our 'human' life while by-passing our 'spiritual' life. Maybe it's kind of like having a big meal and not taking any dessert. The dessert is the favorite part of the meal for many. Makes me think it is the sweetest part. In our spiritual life we need to be sure that we don't by-pass the dessert that we get with knowing who our Savior and Redeemer is. We need to hold them close like we would our most favorite dessert but share with others when we can help make a positive difference in His world.

My favorite desserts are chocolate cake and chocolate chip cookies. When these aren't the choices offered I have been known to pass on dessert. By accepting that Jesus is the one true Son of God and that He is the Savior and Redeemer we can use that choice of dessert at the end of our human life and we can enjoy eternal life with Him at His table. I hope and wish that I can help at least one of God's children enjoy their choice of dessert.

God, I thank you for giving one more day with those that love and care for me and those that I love and care for. I ask that You bless and grant me with the knowledge and wisdom, the power and strength to let others know of Your True Word and to make a difference in Your world. Amen.

Everything that lives and moves about will be food for you. Just as I gave you the green plants, I now give you everything. ~ Genesis 9:3

15

The Reluctant Sergeant
May 23, 2011 at 9:52pm

I watched the movie "When Trumpets Fade" the other
night for the first time and even though the language is a bit
crude at times it is a movie that has some interesting value
to me. We all remember the Battle of the Bulge but not
many remember a terrible time just prior to that battle
which started on the 16th of December, 1944. 24,000 US
soldiers were killed in the fighting on the border between
France and Germany in the Hurtgen Forest.

David Manning is a private in the Army and is fighting in
the Hurtgen Forest in November, 1944. He isn't even a
very good soldier by his own standards but after all, he has
survived. The movie starts when David is carrying a badly
wounded soldier to the rear for medical treatment. These
are the only two survivors of the squad from the action on
the night before. He is selfish and all he wants is to live and
go home, even to the point of when threatened with a court
martial he says he would take that if it would get him out of
the forest and away from the war. When David does get

back to the rear his captain gives him a battlefield promotion to sergeant. David refuses the promotion and asks for a Section 8 so he can be relieved of all duties but this is not allowed by the captain because the captain says that's not possible since Manning has survived he is now the only one capable to lead his squad in the platoon. Sergeant Manning is assigned a group of replacements just brought up to the front.

So many times we are given assignments that we don't want and we are asked to do things we really don't care to do just as Sergeant Manning was ordered to do. Sometimes we even know it is for the better and for the best to get started and to complete our tasks detailed to us. Our Faith asks us to do so many things that many times we put off for a 'better' time to get back to them or just totally refuse to do it at all. We seem to try harder at doing the stuff that is more fun. Go to ball games, out with friends, watching TV or reading a book or maybe even just doing nothing at all.

When Sergeant Manning instructs his green troops to move forward they themselves are reluctant to face the unknown fears in front of them on the battlefield. Sergeant Manning tells them "Nobody dies" if they listen to him and take care of each other. The squad encounters many different and difficult things in the next few days but even though they are alive they start a dislike for their reluctant sergeant. Manning is asked by the captain to take out some 88mm

guns that have been causing many casualties. Manning at
first refuses but then the captain says he will grant the
Section 8 to him if he would volunteer his squad which
David then does. This mission succeeds but with the loss of
all but one of the new replacements and Sergeant Manning.

How many times do we also refuse to do something that we
don't want to do but then do it when we are offered
something we want even more? How many times do we get
self-centered and focus on OUR own desires? Manning's
superiors saw that he was able to do something many of his
peers were unable to do; survive and live. And that he
could lead the new guys in the battle. He was only
interested in himself. He would not "take a bullet" for
anyone as he told his Lieutenant. A day later his Lieutenant
is relieved of his own duties and Manning is awarded
another battlefield promotion to Lieutenant.

In my recovery process I was originally focused on my own
desire to try to cope with what happened. I tried to make
some sense of a senseless incident. So I started writing
these "Notes" on my Facebook profile page. It was a selfish
thing to be totally honest. Then when others started to read
my notes and make comments on them I started writing
more of them. Some said I was an inspiration to them. I
heard many good things and this was good in itself as it
made me feel better and I'm sure has helped with my
cognizance recovery process. I was trying to survive much

the same as David Manning in the Hurtgen Forest. Neither one of us asked for promotions or accolades. In our selfishness we just wanted to go home. We tried to get back to where we once were.

I have no specific reason for this analogy except that when I watched that movie the other night on DVD it made me think of my own issues compared to Sergeant Manning's. I wanted my own Section 8 so I could return to my comfort zone that I had before my injuries affected me. I know that's not possible.

Lieutenant Manning and 3 others go on their own to try to destroy Nazi Panzer tanks that have been inflicting terrible casualties just as the 88's had done the day before. There is now only one of his original replacement soldiers, Private Sanderson, left with him and he says to Manning "Nobody dies, right Lieutenant?" Manning replies "Nobody dies." The movie closes with the private carrying a wounded Lieutenant Manning towards the rear. Manning is grievously hurt and seems to be fading, a Fading Trumpet. Sanderson tells Manning he is "taking you home, Lieutenant. I am taking you home."

I am a 'reluctant' soldier of God's Army. All I wanted was the easy thing; the easy life. Jesus carried me in His arms in those dark days so many months ago. It seems that He has awarded me with a battlefield commission to help lead his soldiers. I pray that He will help me do what He has tasked me to do for Him. When my battles are over I know my Redeemer, Lord Jesus Christ, will be carrying me home.

God, I thank you for giving one more day with those that love and care for me and those that I love and care for. I ask that You bless and grant me with the knowledge and wisdom, the power and strength to let others know of Your True Word and to make a difference in Your world. Amen.

Those who love their life in this world will lose it. Those who care nothing for their life in this world will keep it for eternity. ~ John 12:25

16

"Out Live Your Life" by Max Lucado
June 25, 2011 at 10:49am

Some years back a reporter covering the conflict in
Sarajevo saw a little girl shot by a sniper. The back of her
head had been torn away by the bullet. The reporter threw
down his pad and pencil and stopped being a reporter for a
few minutes. He rushed to the man who was holding the
child and helped them both into his car. As the reporter
stepped on the accelerator, racing to the hospital, the man
holding the bleeding child said, "Hurry, my friend. My
child is still alive."

A moment or two later he pleaded, "Hurry my friend. My
child is still breathing."

A moment later, "Hurry, my friend. My child is still warm."

Finally, "Hurry. Oh my God, my child is getting cold."

By the time they arrived at the hospital, the little girl had
died. As the two men were in the lavatory, washing the

blood off their hands and their clothes, the man turned to the reporter and said, "This is a terrible task for me. I must go tell her father that his child is dead. He will be heartbroken."

The reporter was amazed. He looked at the grieving man and said, "I thought she was your child."

The man looked back and said, "No, but aren't they all our children?"

Indeed. Those who suffer belong to all of us. And if all of us respond, there is hope.

.

17

Don't know Dale Carnegie?

July 6, 2011 at 6:21pm

In a nice little conversation with my son the other day, I made mention of a Dale Carnegie saying and then apologized to Zach for quoting and mentioning Dale Carnegie so many times. Zach then asked who Dale Carnegie was. I was taken aback some by the question as I had thought that most people already knew who he was and what he did.

Dale Carnegie was born in 1888 in Missouri. As a salesman and aspiring actor he traveled to New York and began teaching communications classes at the YMCA. He founded the world famous Dale Carnegie Course in 1912 and authored many books over the next couple of decades including "How To Win Friends and Influence People"

I am a 'graduate' of the Dale Carnegie Sales Advantage course which I took in early 1997. It has been a learning experience that I have recalled many times since I had taken the course. And now I want to impart some of his collections that he had put into "Dale Carnegie's Golden Book" so others that aren't familiar with him and his reflections might be able to build on their own lives such as I have been able to do with that knowledge.

Become a Friendlier Person

1. Don't criticize, condemn or complain.
2. Give honest, sincere appreciation.
3. Arouse in the other person an eager want.
4. Become genuinely interested in other people.
5. Smile.
6. Remember that a person's name is to that person the sweetest and most
important sound in any language.
7. Be a good listener. Encourage others to talk about themselves.
8. Talk in terms of the other person's interests.
9. Make the other person feel important - and do it sincerely.

Win People to Your Way of Thinking

10. The only way to get the best of an argument is to avoid it.
11. Show respect for the other person's opinion. Never say, "You're wrong."
12. If you are wrong, admit it quickly and emphatically.

13. Begin in a friendly way.
14. Get the other person saying "yes, yes" immediately.
15. Let the other person do a great deal of the talking.
16. Let the other person feel that the idea is his or hers.
17. Try honestly to see things from the other person's point of view.
18. Be sympathetic with the other person's ideas and desires.
19. Appeal to the nobler motives.
20. Dramatize your ideas.
21. Throw down a challenge.

Be a Leader

22. Begin with praise and honest appreciation.
23. Call attention to people's mistakes indirectly.
24. Talk about your own mistakes before criticizing the other person.
25. Ask questions instead of giving direct orders.
26. Let the other person save face.
27. Praise the slightest improvement and praise every improvement. Be "hearty in your
approbation and lavish in your praise."
28. Give the other person a fine reputation to live up to.
29. Use encouragement. Make the fault seem easy to correct.
30. Make the other person happy about doing the thing you suggest.

Fundamental Principles for Overcoming Worry

1. Live in "day tight compartments."
2. How to face trouble:
a. Ask yourself, "What is the worst that can possibly happen?"
b. Prepare to accept the worst.
c. Try to improve on the worst.
3. Remind yourself of the exorbitant price you can pay for worry in terms of your health.

Basic Techniques in Analyzing Worry

1. Get all the facts.
2. Weigh all the facts — then come to a decision.
3. Once a decision is reached, act!
4. Write out and answer the following questions:
a. What is the problem?
b. What are the causes of the problem?
c. What are the possible solutions?
d. What is the best possible solution?

Break the Worry Habit Before It Breaks You

1. Keep busy.
2. Don't fuss about trifles.
3. Use the law of averages to outlaw your worries.

4. Cooperate with the inevitable.
5. Decide just how much anxiety a thing may be worth and refuse to give it more.
6. Don't worry about the past.

Cultivate a Mental Attitude that will Bring You Peace and Happiness

1. Fill your mind with thoughts of peace, courage, health and hope.
2. Never try to get even with your enemies.
3. Expect ingratitude.
4. Count your blessings — not your troubles.
5. Do not imitate others.
6. Try to profit from your losses.
7. Create happiness for others.

The Perfect Way to Conquer Worry

1. Pray.

Don't Worry about Criticism

1. Remember that unjust criticism is often a disguised compliment.
2. Do the very best you can.
3. Analyze your own mistakes and criticize yourself.

Prevent Fatigue and Worry and Keep Your Energy and Spirits High

1. Rest before you get tired.
2. Learn to relax at your work.
3. Protect your health and appearance by relaxing at home.
4. Apply these four good working habits:
a) Clear your desk of all papers except those relating to the immediate problem
at hand.
b) Do things in the order of their importance.
c) When you face a problem, solve it then and there if you have the facts necessary
to make a decision.
d) Learn to organize, deputize and supervise.
5. Put enthusiasm into your work.
6. Don't worry about insomnia.

~~~~~~
~~~~~~~~~~~~~~~~~~~~~~~~~~~

I hope everyone can take something from the Dale Carnegie approach to sales and life in general. Carnegie was very spiritual and this was reflected many times over in the 13 week Sales Advantage course I participated in. All of us in the class really got to know each other and we were all able to learn about other people and interacting with them and hopefully were able to make ourselves better at sales and a positive influence in the human race.

18

#41

If someone would ask you the significance of the number 41, what would you say? Many would likely try to name some sports star that they think is wearing that number or used to wear it. Some might say Tom Seaver, Wes Unseld, Eddie Mathews or maybe even that thug from the Detroit Pistons teams from the 1980s, Bill Laimbeer. There might even be a basketball fan out there that would mention Dirk Nowitski of the world champion Dallas Mavericks. I would counter right away with Dave Osborn of the Minnesota Vikings teams of the 70s. A team I loved to watch back then and even now. #41 was the go-to guy at the goal line in those glory years. Didn't matter it seemed at times. Get it close and #41 would leap over the linemen fighting for position in the trenches. Touchdown Minnesota Vikings!!

I was born in 1959 so I got to see many of those great Vikings teams and so many players that I wanted to emulate as I got older and started playing the game of football. A great movie that was released in 1959 is a favorite of mine; Ben Hur. Ben Hur was written by Lew Wallace, a former general in the Union Army during the Civil War. The actual name of the book is "Ben Hur: A Tale of the Christ" and was completed and published in 1880 and is the first book of fiction ever blessed by a Pope. Ben-Hur has long been a movie I cannot watch enough. Charlton Heston is Judah Ben Hur and he earned 11 Academy awards for his performance.

General Lew Wallace often told the story of meeting the well-known agnostic Colonel Robert G. Ingersoll on a train in 1875. For many hours, Ingersoll questioned Wallace about God, heaven and the story of Christ. Wallace said he came away realizing how little he knew about his own religion: "I was ashamed of myself, and make haste now to declare that the mortification of pride I then endured . . . ended in a resolution to study the whole matter." In writing the story, he was able to sort out his own beliefs about God and Christ. He then went on to state: "The Christian world would not tolerate a novel with Jesus Christ its hero, and I knew it. He should not be present as an actor in any scene of my creation. The giving a cup of water to Ben-Hur at the well near Nazareth is the only violation of this rule. . . . I would be religiously careful that every word He uttered should be a literal quotation from one of His sainted biographers." This is why Jesus appears in a cameo role. Wallace says in his autobiography, "When I had finished [the writing], I said to myself with Balthasar, 'God only is so great.' I had become a believer."

The story tells of the adventures of Judah Ben-Hur, Jewish prince and merchant in Jerusalem at the beginning of the 1st century. Ben-Hur's childhood friend Messala arrives back home as an ambitious commanding officer of the Roman legions. They come to realize how much they have changed and now hold very different views and aspirations. During a military parade a tile falls from the roof of Judah's house and barely misses (kills him in the movie) the Roman governor. Although Messala knows that they are not guilty, he condemns the Ben-Hur family. Without trial, Judah is sent to work until death as a Roman galley slave, his mother and sister are thrown into prison and all the family property is confiscated. Through fate and good fortune, Judah survives and manages to return to Jerusalem, to seek revenge against his one-time friend and redeem his family. Judah survives the death march through the desert with the help of an unknown man who gives him water when the long line of slaves stops in a small town and water is allowed to all but Judah Ben-Hur. The unknown man is working in his carpenter's shop and goes outside to watch. He sees the guards refuse Ben Hur a drink and gives Ben Hur some water. When the column of slaves continues onward Judah can't help but turn around many times to look at the strange man who would help a sinner and total stranger. The look in his eyes in the movie tells a great story to any who choose to watch.

Ben Hur is known as #41 in the Roman galley. That is his oar's position below deck. A new commander for the Roman fleet comes aboard as Ben Hur's ship has been assigned to be the flag vessel. The commander goes below to watch his slaves work their oars. In a rest period the commander takes a walk down between the rows of slaves resting with their oars. After a confrontation of sorts between the commander and Ben Hur, the commander instructs the guards to not chain #41 to his oar like the other slaves will be when the fleet does battle with the Macedonian fleet they are likely to encounter soon. This gives Ben Hur a chance to save the commander when the ship is rammed and is sinking. The commander is knocked overboard and Ben Hur dives into the sea to save the heavily armored man. The commander adopts Ben Hur and then grants him his freedom to do whatever he desires so Ben Hur returns to his homeland.

Running in parallel with Ben-Hur's narrative is the unfolding story of Jesus, who comes from the same region and is a similar age, mirroring themes of betrayal, conviction and redemption. Ben-Hur witnesses and is inspired by the rise of the Christ figure and his following who challenge Roman tyranny and talk of keys to a greater kingdom. When Jesus is paraded through town carrying his cross on the way to Calvary Hill, Ben Hur says "I know this man" as he recognizes him as the man who gave him water so many years ago.

While I know the movie version of this story and some of the man who wrote the book, I decided to do a bit of research before writing this piece. I was very surprised to read and learn the reason why General Wallace wrote the book. Reading that "realizing how little he knew about his own religion: "I was ashamed of myself..." I have come to also realize how little I know of my religion and maybe that is part of why God has granted me the additional time in His world. So I can learn more of His greatness and hopefully impart some of that knowledge onto others who care to read my humble stories I have written these past months of recovery.

Jesus gave Judah Ben-Hur water in the desert not only when he was thirsty but when Ben Hur needed hope. Water is a key element found in many stories throughout the Bible, from Noah's ark and the baptism of Jesus to the woman at the well and Moses parting the Red Sea. Many church denominations use water to celebrate the sacrament of baptism and many Christians see water as a symbol of cleansing, redemption, and forgiveness. It was a gift God gave us through his creation and it is crucial to the survival of every living thing just as it was giving Ben Hur hope when there was none to be found. I will endeavor to quench my thirst for His True Word in the time God has granted me.

If you have never seen "Ben Hur" and don't mind watching an old movie that has a great story, I highly recommend this movie.

God, I thank you for giving one more day with those that love and care for me and those that I love and care for. I ask that You bless and grant me with the knowledge and wisdom, the power and strength to let others know of Your True Word and to make a difference in Your world. Amen.

19

Turn The Page .....
December 4, 2011 at 10:11pm

When I was driving to a friends' new shop party last night this old favorite of mine from Bob Seger was playing and even though the song is about a professional singer and how he feels about things and copes with being on the road away from home so for so many days, it made me think of similar things in my own life.

It has been a bit over two years now since I was run down by the hit and run driver. I think I have been able to cope with much of what has been dealt to me in this tragic ordeal. I would like to think that most people who come in contact with me cannot see or even sense some of what goes on in my mind with all of the issues from back then.

**"But your thoughts will soon be wandering
The way they always do
When you're ridin' sixteen hours
And there's nothin' much to do**

And you don't feel much like ridin',
You just wish the trip was through"

The last part of the first verse of the song is what I wish for.
There are probably some that think that I am letting those
travails from 2009 get the best of me. Maybe that they will
eventually consume me. I try very hard and I ask for His
help and blessing to defeat this demon that occupies my
mind.

"Well you walk into a restaurant,
Strung out from the road
And you feel the eyes upon you
As you're shakin' off the cold
You pretend it doesn't bother you
But you just want to explode"

Whether it happens or not I might not ever know. But I do
have thoughts that people look at me when I'm walking
down the sidewalk or at the ballgames and when they
notice my limp they are thinking of how close I was to
leaving the world that God has made for us. And I do just
what Seger says in the last part of the second verse; I
pretend it doesn't bother me but sometimes I want to
explode.

"Most times you can't hear 'em talk,
Other times you can

**All the same old cliches,
"Is that a woman or a man?"
And you always seem outnumbered,
You don't dare make a stand"**

Sometimes I do feel outnumbered. I want things to finally
go "right" for my family. I have questioned investigators. I
have argued with lawyers. I have advised politicians and
lawmakers. I feel I have fought this fight with the best I
have to offer but I now wonder if I dare do much more.

**"Later in the evening
As you lie awake in bed
With the echoes from the amplifiers
Ringin' in your head"**

There are no amplifiers that cause the ringing in my head.
The ringing I hear is from the head trauma from that fateful
night. It is with me from the moment I awake until I am
finally able to drift off to sleep. Sometimes I need to just
get back up and turn the TV on or grab my computer or a
book until I get tired enough to fall asleep.

**"Here I am
On the road again
There I am
Up on the stage
Here I go**

Playin' star again
There I go
Turn the page"

So I will go on my way again down the road to try to learn what all this means to me. I feel God is trying to tell me something and I pray that I will someday be able to turn the page of this book to the last chapter.

God, I thank you for giving one more day with those that love and care for me and those that I love and care for. I ask that You bless and grant me with the knowledge and wisdom, the power and strength to let others know of Your True Word and to make a difference in Your world. Amen.

20

A Time to Judge
December 11, 2011 at 10:31pm

The story of Samson from the Book of Judges has been a focal point of my mind recently. The story of Samson and Delilah has always been one that piqued my interest since I was a youngster. The movie, starring Victor Mature and Hedy Lamarr, was one that I had watched when I was growing up even though it was filmed in 1949 and was already an old movie by the time I had seen it. When the story was told in Sunday school it was once again something that I could not let go of.

Could it be that Samson's story captures my interest because he liked and lived many of the forbidden things of his time? Things that we know are taboo? Seemingly to have fun partying and not having any day-to-day worries?

In Biblical times a judge was a person who was a ruler or a military leader, as well as someone who presided over legal hearings. Samson was born and given the blessing of God to deliver the Israelites from the hands of the Philistines.

But he was not unlike that of a questionable politician in our times. He was easily led to stray from good to evil by his love for women and other sins.

Samson's calling from birth was to begin the deliverance of Israel from Philistine oppression (see Judges 13:5). Reading the account of Samson's life and then his downfall with Delilah, you might tend to think Samson wasted his life. He was a failure. Yet even still, he accomplished his God assigned mission.

We aren't given a list of Samson's failings. We know he had sinned and and that he had recognized this and asked God for His forgiveness after he had told Delilah where is strength had come from and the Philistines cut his hair and rendered him powerless. The Philistines had gouged his eyes out and then put him to work grinding grain and other hard labor in the Gaza prison but they had neglected to keep his hair short. In the prayer Samson asked God to return his strength and with it Samson would kill many of the Philistines as he took his own life in the name of God. This should prove to us that God can use those of us with faith, no matter how imperfect our lives are and have been.

Some time ago when I was visiting Sunset Colony and talking to my friend John Waldner, the minister at the colony, and he was asking about my afflictions and how I was doing and dealing with them. I told John that my faith is real and absolute but that I know there are others whose faith is better and stronger than mine. John replied that maybe it could be that my faith is all that God had given me. That statement has had a profound effect on me since he had told me this.

At the end of his life, blind and humbled, Samson finally realized his utter dependence upon God. He once was blind, but now could see. No matter how far you've fallen away from God, no matter how big you've failed, it's never too late to humble yourself and turn over your dependence upon God. Ultimately, through his sacrificial death, Samson turned his miserable mistakes into victory. Let Samson's example persuade you as it has me ~ it's never too late.

I'm not sure if there are many who would agree to this possibility but it makes me think that maybe, just maybe, the driver of that car that ran me down in that hit and run incident was doing God's will. Maybe that God knew I could help reach others because He knew I would talk of His greatness and help give those around me some hope by seeing this note and reading what I have written about my interpretations of His True Word.

25 While they were in high spirits, they shouted, "Bring out Samson to entertain us." So they called Samson out of the prison, and he performed for them.

When they stood him among the pillars, 26 Samson said to the servant who held his hand, "Put me where I can feel the pillars that support the temple, so that I may lean against them." 27 Now the temple was crowded with men and women; all the rulers of the Philistines were there, and on the roof were about three thousand men and women watching Samson perform. 28 Then Samson prayed to the LORD, "Sovereign LORD, remember me. Please, God, strengthen me just once more, and let me with one blow get revenge on the Philistines for my two eyes." 29 Then Samson reached toward the two central pillars on which the temple stood. Bracing himself against them, his right hand on the one and his left hand on the other, 30 Samson said, "Let me die with the Philistines!" Then he pushed with all his might, and down came the temple on the rulers and all the people in it. Thus he killed many more when he died than while he lived. ~ Judges 16:25-30

God, I thank you for giving one more day with those that love and care for me and those that I love and care for. I ask that You bless and grant me with the knowledge and wisdom, the power and strength to let others know of Your True Word and to make a difference in Your world. Amen.

21

Spending borrowed time

December 17, 2011 at 6:22pm

When you think you know plenty about something and people listen to what you have to say about the subject, you can be called an expert. While I don't think I'm an expert at anything some seem to want to 'listen' to me these days. But I do think I have been given more time in God's world, especially the last couple of years or so. Maybe He wants me to tell others of Him and how I feel about my faith.

As many of you know a little over 2 years ago I was struck down by a hit and run driver who has never been charged. I was on a respirator for a few days after the chopper ride to Merit Care (now Sanford) in Fargo, ND. I have written many things about this ordeal and its aftermath in other notes here on my Facebook profile.

One thing I have not written about and I'm also not very sure how many really know about is how I almost got myself run over this fall out on the harvest at the farm. I knew better but for some reason I left the truck to go talk to

Dad in the grain cart tractor. I need to watch each and every step these days with my walking a question mark after the head injuries from two years ago have caused balance and vision issues. Plus with the harvested cornstalks all around I don't want them to catch my feet and trip me up. I had quickly looked up at Dad as he was nearing the completion of unloading the cart and would soon depart to go catch Scott's combine again. I thought Dad had seen me so I kept going toward the ladder steps to climb up to the cab. The cart tractor has triples these days so there is about a four foot gap between the outside of the tire and the steps. I went around the tires and started reaching for the ladder rail when I heard the tractor click into gear. I was reaching with my left hand for the left rail. For some reason I did not try to turn around or back out of the way of the tires. In doing so I think I would not have been able to get away and would have been run over by the 30,000# tractor. Instead I started moving forward and my left hand grabbed the RIGHT rail and held on with a strength that surprised me. Even as the middle tire clipped me in the rear of the right shoulder I was able to retain my grip. It still amazes me that a cornstalk never grabbed a hold of my feet or that the middle tire didn't pull me under the tractor.

With the left hand firmly holding the right rail I moved my right hand to that rail and released my left so it could go to the left rail while my feet got up on the step. About this time Dad noticed me there and stopped. We both caught our breath a bit. I know this bothered Dad plenty. Even though I told him it was only my fault for the whole thing he said if he had run me over he would have blamed himself.

I can still envision my hand grasping that rail. There is only one reason I didn't go under that tire. The strength that held my hand to that rail wasn't mine. There is no doubt in my mind. I told my best friend and brother in Christ David Brobston about this that night after I returned home. I hadn't told Gretchen yet and refrained from doing so for almost a week. It was kind of embarrassing in that instead of using the two-way radio to talk to Dad I just hopped down from the semi and headed toward his tractor to talk to him. It wasn't a very smart thing to do and the worst part of it would have been the affect it would have had on Dad if it would have been a worse result.

Many have told me I should write a book. Some, like Terrill Sorenson, Sara Sorenson and Holly Hoffman have told me I should talk to people such as a motivational type speaker would do. I struggle with these things. My memory isn't all that good and at times my speech suffers, especially when I am tired or excited. I told Pastor Dave that if I ever could do such things I had a title: **Spending Borrowed Time**. Because each moment I have on this earth is borrowed time. I mentioned to Pastor Terrill that maybe it was time I started paying on the principal.

I will continue to learn from my days on this earth and someday maybe I will be able to understand why God keeps giving me moments with those here that I love and care for. Someday maybe He will be able to say I have done something good in His world and have made a difference to those who seek the knowledge of the Word.

God, I thank you for giving one more day with those that love and care for me and those that I love and care for. I ask that You bless and grant me with the knowledge and wisdom, the power and strength to let others know of Your True Word and to make a difference in Your world. Amen.

A friend loves at all times,
and a brother is born for a time of adversity. ~ Proverbs 17:17

22

Tebow Faith + Faith in Tebow
January 15, 2012 at 10:04pm

With Tim Tebow's Denver Broncos season ending last night in the loss to the Patriots I decided it was time to post my thoughts about Tim Tebow, Tebow's Faith, Tebowing, etc., etc.

I think it is time for the Tebow bashers to crawl away to where they belong. Why is it that when a guy like Tebow comes along professing his Faith gets chastised top to bottom, front to back, side to side and then the bashers relish the thought to do it once again. Do these Tebow bashers have the same thoughts about moronic mistakes such as that made by Plaxico Burress? Beam about the exploits of Ray Lewis on the field while forgetting about his gang life and murder suspicion before big-time football? Or how about the Rae Carruth type people in our world? Carruth is the NFL football player who was found guilty of conspiring in the murder of his girlfriend that he had gotten pregnant back in 2001.

I have been a Tebow fan for many years. I had been a Tebow fan for some time when I was hospitalized in Merit Care in Fargo back in November of 2009 when I was struck down in the vehicle versus pedestrian hit and run incident. Because of the brain injury I was suffering from as a part of the result of that terrible ordeal, when I emerged from my coma and was deemed ready to start therapy I was told I should keep a "Memory Log" to help me regain some memory functions. I posted in late November of 2009 **"Go Tim Tebow. Tebow is a winner but he got beat by Ark today"** in reference to Arkansas beating his team that day.

Tim Tebow is for sure not as polished of a quarterback as Aaron Rodgers, Drew Brees, Tom Brady. But he is a winner. And it doesn't matter if we are talking about on the field or off the field. He flat out wins. Some say he isn't a real QB. That the QB position is for passers, especially those who do it in style like the three mentioned earlier in this paragraph. I heartily disagree. A true QB leads his team. A true QB runs the offense in the way his coaching staff has directed him and he does it with the players the coaching staff and in the NFL, with the players the front office has provided him.

Tebow does his job with the abilities God has provided him and is not shy about proclaiming the gifts that God bestowed upon him. 1 Peter 4:11 says: **"If anyone speaks, he should do it as one speaking the very words of God. If anyone serves, he should do it with the strength God**

provides, so that in all things God may be praised through Jesus Christ. To him be the glory and the power for ever and ever. Amen."

By now many have probably heard the story of Tim Tebow's parents being missionaries in the Philippines before he was born. His mother was afflicted with an intestinal parasite which made her very sick and she was given powerful medicines before anyone knew she was pregnant. The doctors told the soon-to-be parents that the fetus likely would be severely damaged and recommended an abortion. But his mother wouldn't think of that as an option. She prayed to God **"If you will give us a son, we'll name him Timothy and we'll make him a preacher."** She almost lost the baby four different times and spent the last two months on bed rest. Her youngest son is indeed a preacher. He preaches in prisons, makes hospital visits, and serves with his father's ministry in the Philippines. This is the Tim Tebow that I think is a better role model than so many other of the professional sport athletes and movie star types.

I am one who feels that the Tebow bashers need to look in the mirror and see how they can change their life to help make God's world a better one for all of us to live in.

God, I thank you for giving one more day with those that love and care for me and those that I love and care for. I ask that You bless and grant me with the knowledge and wisdom, the power and strength to let others know of Your True Word and to make a difference in Your world. Amen.

23

Do Facebook "Pokes" get your attention?
February 7, 2012 at 9:09am

Some that read this "Note" of mine already know what a Facebook "Poke" is. Not exactly sure how I got started doing the poking thing on FB or who helped get me started but I get amused and have some fun "poking" around every once in awhile. Recently I got into a "Poke" war with some of my FB Mob Wars friends on a Sunday afternoon and I think there were a bunch of us from around the world having fun clicking and poking each other and I think we all were amused by our antics. It got our attention and provided some entertainment along the way. I was reminded of this in my restlessness last night and my poor ability to sleep.

Does God "Poke" us from time to time? In His own way I'm guessing He does. After logging into Facebook this morning and noting how many "Pokes" I had waiting for me (7) it made me stop and think about the way God gets our attention. I asked myself this and went to Google to find the answer. I found this:

"By means of their suffering, He rescues those who suffer. For He gets their attention through adversity." - Job 36:15

Did that get **YOUR** attention? As much as it did mine? WOW.....This Bible verse helps me to try to understand how and what happened to me a couple of years ago. It's no secret I had to go through some suffering and adversity in those afflictions. Still do and always will.

I also found this on the internet from Pastor Eddie Ildefonso:

Have you ever had an important message to tell someone, but you could not get that person's undivided attention? Perhaps you thought, maybe I should try to communicate this at some later time, but the urgency pressed you to keep trying. God's messages to us are always important and timely, and they deserve our complete attention. Why? He has charted a perfect course for our life. Knowing the future completely, He sees when our own plans do not align with His. When we begin to wander from His course, He will take numerous measures to capture our attention and protect us from harm.

All too often, the Lord's wisdom is muffled by the clamor of daily life. Sometimes we start out with God's agenda but get so far ahead of Him that we can no longer hear His voice. Preferring to do things our own way, we lose contact with our only true Guide.

Unfortunately, we are not always spiritually alert. For such situations, God has a number of ways to help us take notice.

Pastor Ildefonso also writes:

One of the simplest ways God gets our attention is by making us restless. When King Ahasueruas was unable to sleep, he ordered that the royal record books be read. As a result, he discovered his life had been saved by Esther's uncle. In wanting to honor Mordecai, the king unwittingly set in motion a chain of events that caused Haman's planned annihilation of the Jews to be exposed. (Esther 6, 7) The Jewish nation was spared because the king was alerted when God gave him a restless spirit. If you experience a restlessness deep within, something you sense but cannot quite identify, the wise thing to do is stop and pray, "Lord, are You trying to say something to me?" God does not work the same way in everyone's life, but I believe His primary method for getting my attention is by giving me a restlessness to show I need a change of direction. As I reread my old journal entries, a pattern emerges each time God was about to move me from one ministry opportunity to another, I would become very restless for a few months.

This is a very gentle method God uses to correct our course.

God has "Poked" me many times and I did not respond. I am trying my best now to let Him know that He now has my attention.

God, I thank you for giving one more day with those that love and care for me and those that I love and care for. I ask that You bless and grant me with the knowledge and wisdom, the power and strength to let others know of Your True Word and to make a difference in Your world. Amen.

24

What is fear?

February 12, 2012 at 12:36pm

Not sure why this popped into my skull today but I'm having a hard time getting it moved out so I have decided to write about it.

We all have fears or at least if we have a sound mind we do. We might laugh at those who fear of making a fool out of themselves. Such as messing up in a sporting event or doing something foolish in our lives. Maybe talking behind the back of someone and they find out about it. Some fear not having enough money or bad health and many variations of health. Some fear of not being noticed or they fear of not being important enough. Bad accidents and things like this also come to my mind in this regard. We all probably have some type of fear when it comes to those we love and care for and would like to think we can and would do anything in our powers to be able to keep them safe. We might fear death.

I think I can honestly say I don't think I do have the fear of death. I would like to think I am comfortable in the sense knowing I have lived my life in a way that I don't have a lot of regrets. Some years ago when my son was involved in Cub Scouts they planned a night out at the local state park lake area campground. When the youngsters were in their sleeping bags in the gathering of tents us Dads sat around the campfire having a cold brew ..... or two. The conversation was interesting to say the least as many who have experienced this type of situation can relate to. Somebody asked if anybody could do so, would they do something differently? If they could go back in time with the possibility of changing that event, would they? Oh there were many who talked of doing this thing or that thing. Of working harder on the basketball court, of dating that hot cheerleader instead of just wishing she would notice you. Of course there was talk of things that it seems only dreams are made of. When it came my time to speak I'm not sure many believed me when I said I wouldn't change a thing. I explained my thought with the rationale that since I like movies and some of these movies are science fiction movies such as "Time Cop" where it is explained that if you change any part of history ripples are cast into the time of your life that can totally change any and all things with your current and future life. I don't want that.

I went on to talk of why I feel that way since I was on my soapbox and the guys seemed to actually be listening to me.

I told of my morning of 19 March, 1999 when I was in the hospital with wires hooked up to me and in the midst of a major heart attack. I could see my pulse rate escalating on the monitor. I watched the blood pressure dropping. Pulse 156 and rising. BP 92/46 and dropping. Then the nurses noticed I was watching the monitor and one of them turned it so I could not see it anymore. So I looked straight ahead at the wall of the hospital room. There was a lot of pain with the proverbial white elephant sitting on my chest but what upset me the most was it was hard to breathe. The crucifix on the wall caught my attention even though I'm not Catholic. Next to the crucifix was a clock. I noticed the time and even though that was almost 13 years ago I remember these events with a clarity that some cannot understand. The time was 7:39 in the morning and I was thinking "Huh.....so this is what it is like to check out" and then wondering if this was the room my banker and friend (Duke Nietert) of my Dad had been in the day before when he had died of a heart attack (it was...) and I had seen the chopper leave town that morning wondering if I knew who it was carrying.

I knew I couldn't go back and do anything different in my life. I couldn't undo anything I had done. I couldn't eat less steak, drink less beer. Or more for that matter. My life, as I knew it anyway, was over. I was entering some new part of my existence. I didn't know how long that newness was going to last. When I would be starting the next level of whatever, where ever I was. It didn't matter. The only thing that did matter in my human life was I might not be able to do things with my kids that I wanted to do. And I might be standing before the Supreme Judge at any moment and what was I to say if He asked me how I had lived my life? Would I be able to say I had done some of His work? Not enough I knew and then 10 years later I am still wondering how I could do enough.

Today's first lesson was from 2Kings 5:1-14 about Naaman and his leprosy and having to deal with a servant instead of Elisha the prophet. He thought he was important enough to be noticed and warrant full attention. The servant told Naaman "Go wash yourself seven times in the Jordan, and your flesh will be restored and you will be cleansed." 2Kings 5:10.

"I thought that he would surely come out to me..." says verse 11. Naaman was the commander of king Aram and he was a proud man. He felt disrespected by Elisha and maybe Naaman didn't want to show his terrible leprosy sores to the public by doing what the servant had told him. Naaman's own servant chastised him in a way by saying if the prophet himself would have said to go to the Jordan he would have so why not since it was the prophet's own words? Naaman was humbled and went and dipped himself seven times in the Jordan and his skin was returned to a young boy-like condition.

I will try harder to humble myself and to keep from being a man too proud of himself to do what is right in His world.

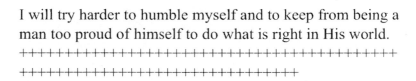

Even though I walk through the valley of the shadow of death, I will fear no evil, for you are with me; your rod and your staff, they comfort me. (Psalm 23:4)

For I am the Lord, your God, who takes hold of your right hand and says to you, Do not fear; I will help you. (Isaiah 41:13)

Moses answered the people, "Do not be afraid. Stand firm and you will see the deliverance the Lord will bring you today. The Egyptians you see today you will never see again." (Exodus 14:13)

Be strong and courageous. Do not be afraid or terrified because of them, for the Lord your God goes with you; he will never leave you nor forsake you. (Deuteronomy 31:6)

For God gave us not a spirit of fearfulness; but of power and love and discipline. (2 Timothy 1:7)

The Lord is my light and my salvation--whom shall I fear? The Lord is the stronghold of my life--of whom shall I be afraid? (Psalm 27:1)

But the angel said to her, "Do not be afraid, Mary, you have found favor with God." (Luke 1:30)

But the angel said to them, "Do not be afraid. I bring you good news of great joy that will be for all the people." (Luke 2:10)

So we say with confidence, "The Lord is my helper; I will not be afraid. What can Man do to me?" (Hebrews 13:6)

Peace I leave with you; my peace I give you. I do not give to you as the world gives. Do not let your hearts be troubled and do not be afraid. (John 14:27)

God, I thank you for giving one more day with those that love and care for me and those that I love and care for. I ask that You bless and grant me with the knowledge and wisdom, the power and strength to let others know of Your True Word and to make a difference in Your world. Amen.

25

It's just a number....
February 29, 2012 at 9:56pm

How many times have we heard this expression? Especially when in the context of experiencing a birthday? Birthdays these days really don't mean much to me anymore. Although I have had some traumatic issues near my last "Big" birthdays. A few months prior to my 40th back in 1999 I had my heart attacks and related incidents. A few months after my 50th birthday was also a near demise as that was when I was hit by the hit and run driver. Maybe I need to wrap myself in bubble-wrap when my 60th rolls around. ;-)

There are plenty of instances that the Bible speaks of numbers. Significant numbers are 1, 2, 3, 4, 5, 6, 7, 10, 12, 40, 50, and 70. I will cite some evidence but this is by no means a complete list:

1) There is one body and one spirit Ephesians 4:4-6
2) Sharper than any double-edged sword from Hebrews 4:12

3) The Holy Trinity

4) The four winds Matthew 24:31

5) The 5 books of Moses and of course, the 5 loaves of bread

6) Man was created in the 6th day

7) Perfection....the number 7 is used 562 times in the Bible

10) The 10 Commandments

12) Represents the church and God's authority. Jesus had 12 disciples, and there were 12 tribes of Israel.

40) It rained for 40 days during the flood. Moses spent 40 years in the desert. Jesus fasted for 40 days.

50) Pentecost occurred 50 days after Christ's resurrection

70) Represents human leadership and judgment. Moses appointed 70 elders

We all have favorite numbers and numbers we are suspicious of too. The first locker combination I ever had back in 6th grade was 20-30-6. Before I was injured if I dialed a phone number 2 times or more, I had a good chance to retain that phone number. We probably had a number that we were identified with in school and as tax day nears we all know that our Social Security number or our Employer Identification Number are what we file under and that is how the IRS identifies us. If we were or are sports fanatics we have a favorite number or we can identify our favorite player by his or her number. We want our college football or basketball team to get the #1 rating and to win the season's championship so we can say "We're #1! We're #1!" to all of those that will listen to us.

Most would say that the number 7 is a lucky number. Gamblers like 7 and 11. 7/11 can be a great place to get a refreshment and other condiments when we are away from home. 9/11 is a solemn number for Americans and many of our friends in Canada, the UK and other places around the world.

The number 7 has meant something else to me the past couple of years or so. The intersection nearest to where I was hit by that car back on 14 November, 2009 is the intersection of 7th Street and 7th Avenue. I cannot make this up. An unbeliever and skeptics will say it was the lucky 7 and 7 that helped me survive that incident. I don't think so. I think that was coincidence. I think it is the Harmon Killebrew number that is the key to my survival on this earth. Killebrew wore number 3 for the Twins. 3 for the Triune God. That's why I am still able to be around.

I will look forward to counting my blessings as my days on His earth go forward.

God, I thank you for giving one more day with those that love and care for me and those that I love and care for. I ask that You bless and grant me with the knowledge and wisdom, the power and strength to let others know of Your True Word and to make a difference in Your world. Amen.

Go therefore and make disciples of all nations, baptizing them in the name of the Father and of the Son and of the Holy Spirit~ Matthew 28:19

For there are three that testify ~ John 5:7

The Spirit and the water and the blood; and these three agree ~ John 5:8

26

Baseball + softball + summer + family & friends = AWESOME
May 27, 2012 at 12:09pm

I love the game of baseball.

I admit it and sometimes that love has been a fault of mine. Back in 1994 I got so terribly upset with Major League baseball when they went on strike in August and even the World Series wasn't played. I wasn't going to ever return to the game and stayed pretty much away for most of 10 years. I eventually got back into watching the Twins play when they were pretty much a perennial playoff team.

I grew up in a family where we had games many times during the summer. All of us played, Dad, Mom, my 3 sisters and 2 brothers although Scott didn't come along to this world until 1967. So he wasn't able to do much for a few years. We would wait for Dad to get done with the farm work so we could gather around the kitchen table for supper and then scoot outside to start playing. We would play in front of the corn granary because it had thick wooden doors that would always remain closed and that made for a great backstop. We would use that pair of wooden doors basically as a catcher at times. Of course those early years we played with a larger softball that Dad always called a "kitten-ball" and we would play until after the yard light would come on and the mosquitoes would be out. But boy, did we have fun.

As Roger and I got older we made our own game of ball. We would play against each other and this was with a baseball instead of the softball. Roger could throw harder than I could but I could hit him better with my throws. ;-) We beat the crap out of that set of wooden doors. I think they are still splintered to this day although a few coats of white paint might have filled in the cracks over the years. The game we made was an interesting one. Since we were both right-handed you could swing away left-handed but only bunt right-handed. And you had to get to second base to get a hit. You could record an out by throwing the ball at the runner and hitting them. Yes!!! Roger became a much better left-handed hitter than I ever did. We both developed decent abilities to bunt with this game strategy. As Scott got older he would be designated hitter for both teams. He got a LOT of at-bats with this game of ours. He basically batted every other time for each team.

One year our parents informed Roger and me that if we wanted to we could play midget and peewee baseball in Claremont. Of course our eyes lit up with this possibility. Roger was young enough to play peewees but also old enough and good enough to warrant some midget time too. That was in 1972. I remember the year because I batted 1.000 that year, the only year I did so. Our first game that year was against Langford in Claremont. I didn't start the game but came in later. In my first at-bat I hit a 37 hopper past the 2nd baseman into right field for a single. Soon the game was over and we went home. A day or so later I flipped my mini-bike and broke my left arm so was done for the year.

The next year Roger and I were both on the midget team. He batted lead-off and I was at the bottom third of the line-up. While Roger fell into a cold snap hitting I found a good stroke and was hitting well. Our coaches, Larry Vietmeier and Ray Nelson switched Roger and me around in the order so I finished the year in the lead-off spot.

Then in 1974 Claremont fielded a Teeners team for the first time ever. Larry Vietmeier took on the coaching slot here while Ray stayed with the midgets. I again did well enough to warrant the lead-off spot. I remember playing Rich Zimney with his Fidel Castro flat-topped olive-drab cap pitching for Ferney. We went south to Ferney to play them and I had a good day for sure. I got on base in the first inning, stole second on the first pitch and then third on the next pitch. When I got up from sliding into 3rd, Larry called time and talked in a low manner to me that he hadn't given me the steal sign to come to third base. I told Larry I knew that but the 3rd baseman was playing up in front of the base a few steps so I just took off. I didn't have the guts to tell him I didn't know the signs. And this was about half way through the season! I just knew nobody could throw me out so I took off.....all year long too. Although after that Ferney game I played a little more close to the vest with stealing, at least 3rd base anyway.

That was also a year that gave me my first sports injury, my first ambulance ride. Tournament time in Frederick. The midget team was in a tournament in Bristol so Dad went with Roger to Bristol and Mom to Frederick. Our first game Brett Gibbs, normally our center-fielder while I was in leftfield, was pitching that game so I slid over to center. It was a very hot, very windy day. First inning the opposing team, I think it was Frederick but not sure since it was a tournament, got the bases loaded with nobody out. The next hitter hit a lazy sinking type line-drive toward center. I came running in, secondbaseman Brad Hanson went drifting out, we both were evidently calling for the ball but with the wind we never heard the other guy call out. We smacked heads and pretty hard too. I was wearing wire-rimmed glasses with real glass lenses. My right lense shattered and the glasses cut open my right eyebrow making for a lot of blood. We only had brought 10 players to the tournament and both Brad and I were carted off the field and loaded into the ambulance even though Brad insisted he could still play. I was told we borrowed a player from the other team to finish that game and to play the next game. I think Brad and I both had concussions and I got a whale of a shiner and a bunch of stitches. Still have the scar too.

We were to play at Eureka a short time later. Larry was concerned about me playing so soon after the head bump. He asked my folks and me but I wanted to play and did play getting a couple of hits and scoring a couple of runs too. I held off on stealing bases that game though. That was my one and only year of Teener ball as the Legion team was going to be short-handed and Brett Gibbs, Brad Hanson, Mark Cutler and I were moved up to Legion to play with some of the guys who we had played ball with the past few years anyway. Older guys like Loren Cutler and Mark Hoines. (Sorry Mark,,,,I had to get that jab into this note of mine....lol). Not an eventful year to say the least although I was playing leftfield in Ipswich when Curt Cutler picked 3 guys off first with his fabulous left-handed move. I might add that Curt did this in the first inning. Yup, all 3 outs via pick-offs at first. I also remember dropping a fly ball in left. I was embarrassed to say the least.

A new coach in the bicentennial year of 1976. Winston "Windy" Feser was our coach. He tried hard to make me into an infielder and a pitcher. That was a miserable failure. I always preferred playing out on the green grass. Windy had different thoughts about our great game. He preferred coaching us from the firstbase coaching box. I think he wanted to be there because so many of us were right-handed hitters. OoooooKkkkkkkkk.......

We always rode the Legion's bus to Legion games back then before Windy drove it in front of a truck or something and wrecked it going to a Teener game or something like that. Anyway, we went to Cresbard for a 9-inning night game as they had lights and some towns, like Claremont didn't. I was batting 5th in those days. I think here again Windy was trying to make me into a power hitter. In the first inning I got up to the plate with two on, two out. Craig Connell was the pitcher. I hit a high fly to right-center. I knew I hit it good so took off out of the box as fast as I could go. When I got close to second the umpire was signaling a homerun. My first ever!! Another first happened for me that game. As I said earlier, Windy liked coaching from firstbase. I got a single, stole second and was on thirdbase with Loren Cutler at bat. Brett Gibbs was coaching third. Windy gave the squeeze sign. Brett looked at me and quietly asked if I had the sign. Both of us knew that it was questionable if Loren had seen it but our baseball fundamentals told us if he didn't and I wasn't able to score, it was his fault and not ours. So when the pitcher made his first move towards home, I took off. I got closer, and closer and closer.....and Loren kept his bat held in place. Nope, he wasn't bunting. He missed the sign. I barreled into home sliding head-first. I don't think the catcher had a clue I was coming. So officially I got a steal of home. lol

The next 15 years or so I bounced around from my last year in Legion, to town team, to slow-pitch, to town team again, back to slow-pitch. Throw in one year, 1981 to be exact, that I played fast-pitch in Britton. Now that was a game! One memorable time was when we were playing Hecla. Tuffy Dinger, one of the best fast-pitch hurlers in the state, was throwing for Hecla. I was batting lead-off. I dropped down a bunt for a single to start the game. I stole second and went to third on an infield out, scored on a fly ball. We won the game 1-0 with Tuffy throwing a one-hitter, my bunt single. Nice.

Also in the mix of this 15 years was my coaching the Britton Legion team in 1984-1985. In '85 we went to State and this was a big highlight of my sports life. My first game as a coach Todd Ramsey pitched for us over in Webster. We got beat 1-0 in 10 innings with Todd throwing all ten innings. We were decent that year but fell to Webster in the district. Before the next season got going, Jim Bjerke, the coach for Clark, called me late the winter prior to the season to see if we wanted to play in a July tournament. I said yes we would. Then he said it was his goal to have 8 teams in the tourney and those same 8 teams he expected to also have in Clark in August for the State "B" Legion championship. I have to tell everyone that he was 7 out of 8 that year. Jim knew his baseball. Members of that team are always in my mind, even decades later. Brian Rabenberg, Bill Meyer, Scott Christenson, Troy Anenson, Jerry Gangle, Brian Hansen, Alan Wolff, Chad Haaland, Jeff Planteen, Steve Young and Corey Brubakken were the 11 members of that year's team. Only 11 players that year but a very dedicated and fun bunch to work with. A better coach could have taken them further but this one had a lot of fun.

I returned to amateur ball in 1991 with the Britton squad led by Wally Steiner. It was a real chore to do this after playing softball for so many years. My limited skills had eroded plenty. It was so bad that I asked Wally if he would help me by hitting fly balls to me for a couple of evenings. Wally had decided to play me (maybe I should say "hide me" ...) in right field and there is a different way the ball comes off the bat when you're in rightfield than when you're in left. I totally sucked and was able to recognize the fact that I needed help and a lot of it. Wally met me at the baseball field in Britton and brought both Jory Steiner and David Bohl to help out. They shagged my lame throws from the outfield and caught the relay throws for Wally. Lots of bugs. Lots of sweat. But I gained some of that experience I seemed to have lost on the softball field. We had lots of fun that year. A road trip to Granite Falls, MN and then to Valley Fair was a great time.

The next year was one of the most fun baseball years I ever had as a player. A memorable game for me early that year was when we played Groton here in Britton. The first game of the double-header Wally was pitching and Wally pretty much always seemed to want me as his left-fielder. Wally got into a spot of trouble in the first inning. With two guys on and two outs, Brian Schuring, a left-handed hitter, came up. Usually a pull hitter so I shaded a bit toward Brian Rabenberg in center as Brian moved a bit more towards Roger Christenson in right. Schuring hit a shot that was going to be a gapper between Rabenberg and me. Both of us got on our horses to run the ball down. I glanced over at Brian and hollered a question to him asking if he could get it. Brian said no, go for it. So I knew Brian would be backing me up if I did. I dove full extension at that ball snaring it in my glove. With a little tuck and roll to make sure I kept a good grip of the ball I came up with the ball and glove high in the air. Everybody was high-fiving me and slapping me on the back for the circus like catch. I got up to Snoot and asked "Hey Snoot! What ya think of that?" Wally replied, "What the **** do you think I have you out there for?" Everyone that heard Snoot laughed and we went on to play a fun game with that Groton team. It started out a bit rocky but the team jelled late. What a great time to come together as a team! We earned the right to go to the State tournament and then proceeded to knock off a couple of teams that probably saw all of us oldsters barely able to move, with our weak outfield arms and a poor set of statistics as an easy bunch to send on their way home. We beat Crofton, NE in a thrilling 1-0 game and then beat a couple more teams by slight margins to draw us into the semi-finals. We got beat by a Vermillion team that was loaded with plenty of college level players but we gave them an 11 inning tussle with a couple of comebacks to keep the game going. Members of that tournament team were Wally Steiner, Marty Weismantle, Doug Jorgensen, Brian Rabenberg, David Brobston, TJ Just, Roger Christenson, Randy Stanley, Brett Sime, Loren "Dell" Nelson, Chris Bruce and myself. I'm thinking I'm missing a player or two but can't remember at this time. We "drafted" 3 players from District teams to have on our roster for the State tournament and they were Dan Karst from Groton, BJ Scheafbauer from Mobridge and Corey Fiedler of Selby. Wally was the glue that held that team together that year and provided a spark that moved us forward. Always full of encouragement and a zest for the game unequalled by anyone I have ever known.

I hung up my spikes after that season, never to put them on again. I rarely lifted a ball to throw again either. After my shoulder surgery in November of 2010 I purchased a Pitch-Back Net like Roger and I used to have growing up. I set it in my backyard to try to gain some strength and flexibility back. I was able to hit the net on maybe 60% of my throws and these were only from 25-30 feet away. It was a pitiful sight to say the least.

With Memorial Day upon us we are tasked to remember those that are no longer with us. Mostly for our war dead and those that served in our military but we should stop and remember those like Wally and Chris who have left this world all too soon. It's a good day to play 2. Rest in peace my friends Wally and Chris.

27

Fundamentals: Hit the cut-off man

June 16, 2012 at 4:53pm

Like many other people, I have some pet peeves. They range from leaving closet doors open, to dust on the dash in the vehicles, leaving the toilet lid up and so on. Yes, I frown on seeing the toilet lid open. As men, we all have been chastised when we have left the toilet seat up so why is it supposedly OK when the female persuasion leaves the lid up?!!??

In my previous note I told of my enjoyment of baseball and some of the reasons why I love the game. I have a pet peeve regarding baseball and the way it is played these days. It doesn't seem to matter what level of baseball either which is even more irritating to me. Poor base-running, poor bat discipline and poor outfield play are some of those irritations I am speaking of here. When you're at the major league level I feel there is absolutely no reason to get picked off first base 6-7-8 times in a season like Denard Span of the Twins did not long ago. Not being able to get a bunt down is another head-shaker, especially on the suicide squeeze play. You hang that runner coming in from third totally out to dry when you don't make contact, even a foul is acceptable in this situation. I mean, all you have to do is CATCH the ball with your bat. Get your head right down next to the place where the ball will meet your bat. Sounds simple doesn't it? Well it is if you are prepared properly to utilize your fundamentals taught in your early days of playing the game.

But as a former outfielder nothing really gets my goat any more than poor outfield play. Poor positioning, bad angles, not knowing the hitter's tendencies and poor concentration are the foundation of not paying attention to playing the game with proper fundamentals. But one of the easiest staples of outfield play that is ignored or not respected very well is missing the cut-off man. If he isn't where you're supposed to expect him, then he is the one guilty of poor fundamentals. Keep the hitter at first if you don't have a chance to throw out the lead runner. Keep him at second if you cannot get the runner going home. You just might save your team a run that can be crucial later in the game.

You don't have to have a rocket or a cannon for an arm to throw runners out either. Proper set-up and a quick and accurate throw to the infield is a better approach than winding up and throwing a laser into the infield. That frozen rope to the infielder might look cool but when you're winding up for that throw the runner is running away from you trying to advance. Much better to have him try to beat your throw than trying to have your throw beat the runner.

In a way, much the same can be said about our Faith. We better have good fundamentals or the other team might score more than we would like them to and can afford to have them score. Jesus is the cut-off man. God is at Home where we need to focus our fundamentals. Jesus knows where He needs to be on the field. We need to know where He is so we can make the proper plays. He will always be there. We need to trust Him to take us Home to God. We need to get it right. We need to CATCH His Word. Keep our head close to the ball. He is always there waiting for us and our efforts.

And when it comes to prayers and praying, all prayers are answered. The answers might not be what **we** want but they are answered. We must take the answers to our prayers and move forward and climb that hill in front of us. It's not always an easy hike to the top of the mountain but the sight at the top will be worth the effort if we let it and understand the fundamentals of our Faith.

28

Armor Up
July 18, 2012 at 8:29pm

2 Corinthians 12:2-10 ~~~~~ That was one of the scripture messages a few weeks ago. Paul is fast becoming a favorite writer of mine and this just reinforced that thought.

I know a man in Christ who fourteen years ago was caught up to the third heaven. Whether it was in the body or out of the body I do not know—God knows. And I know that this man—whether in the body or apart from the body I do not know, but God knows— was caught up to paradise and heard inexpressible things, things that no one is permitted to tell. I will boast about a man like that, but I will not boast about myself, except about my weaknesses. Even if I should choose to boast, I would not be a fool, because I would be speaking the truth. But I refrain, so no one will think more of me than is warranted by what I do or say, or because of these surpassingly great revelations. Therefore, in order to keep me from becoming conceited, I was given a thorn in my flesh, a messenger of Satan, to torment me. Three times I pleaded with the Lord to take it away

from me. But he said to me, "My grace is sufficient for you, for my power is made perfect in weakness. "
Therefore I will boast all the more gladly about my weaknesses, so that Christ's power may rest on me. That is why, for Christ's sake, I delight in weaknesses, in insults, in hardships, in persecutions, in difficulties. For when I am weak, then I am strong.

Most that know me, especially my family and those who are familiar with circumstances surrounding me health wise the past 13 years can relate to some of what I think and feel after those afflictions. 3 heart attacks in 17 days back in March of 1999 followed by the hit and run incident from 2009 and now my newest battle with CLL, a form of Leukemia. I have told many that it's just another hill to climb and I put my mountain boots on each day when I get up. No hill for a climber. I probably should have been run over in October last year by a tractor during the harvest. I wrote of this in a December "Note" titled "Spending Borrowed Time" and I tell that it wasn't my hand that was the strongest that day.

Paul writes* about choosing not to boast about what he has seen. He doesn't want to be thought of as being conceited. But when he does talk about himself he tells of his weaknesses. He talks of a messenger from Satan who comes to torment him. Paul asks God on three different occasions to take the demon away. But God tells him "My grace is sufficient for you, for my power is made perfect in weakness."

I had "tagged" people in my earliest notes but quit doing that part way through 2010. I did not want people to think I was conceited in my writing. Another shade of Paul you might say. With this recent health issue I have told some that it seems to me that Satan wants this stuff to happen. That he wants me to question God why He is letting these things strike me. That Satan wants me to curse God and to look away from Him. But each time I have had something bad happen, my Faith has grown. It has gotten stronger and more resolute. I have gotten more vocal to those around me about Faith and God. I have become more sure of a just reward waiting for us if we live like Job did.

Sometimes, when bad things happen to people, they blame God for this happening to them. They feel that if God is really all knowing and in charge and a good God, why would He do these things? They don't understand the story of Job. Job was blameless and upright. One day the angels came to present themselves before the Lord, and Satan also came with them. The Lord said to Satan, "Where have you come from?" Satan answered the Lord, "From roaming throughout the earth, going back and forth on it." Then the Lord said to Satan, "Have you considered my servant Job? There is no one on earth like him; he is blameless and upright, a man who fears God and shuns evil." "Does Job fear God for nothing?" Satan replied. "Have you not put a hedge around him and his household and everything he has? You have blessed the work of his hands, so that his flocks and herds are spread throughout the land. But now stretch out your hand and strike everything he has, and he will surely curse you to your face."

The Lord said to Satan, "Very well, then, everything he has is in your power, but on the man himself do not lay a finger." Then Satan went out from the presence of the Lord.

One day when Job's sons and daughters were feasting and drinking wine at the oldest brother's house, a messenger came to Job and said, "The oxen were plowing and the donkeys were grazing nearby, and the Sabeans attacked and made off with them. They put the servants to the sword, and I am the only one who has escaped to tell you!" While he was still speaking, another messenger came and said, "The fire of God fell from the heavens and burned up the sheep and the servants, and I am the only one who has escaped to tell you!" While he was still speaking, another messenger came and said, "The Chaldeans formed three raiding parties and swept down on your camels and made off with them. They put the servants to the sword, and I am the only one who has escaped to tell you!" While he was still speaking, yet another messenger came and said, "Your sons and daughters were feasting and drinking wine at the oldest brother's house, when suddenly a mighty wind swept

in from the desert and struck the four corners of the house.
It collapsed on them and they are dead, and I am the only
one who has escaped to tell you! "

At this, Job got up and tore his robe and shaved his head.
Then he fell to the ground in worship and said:
"Naked I came from my mother's womb,   and naked I
will depart. The Lord gave and the Lord has taken away;
    may the name of the Lord be praised."

In all this, Job did not sin by charging God with
wrongdoing.
~~~~~~

Job did not blame God. He did not curse God. And Job
continued to praise God. Job pretty much lost everything in
a day. As it is written, Job got the news of one terrible thing
after another from a messenger and "…while he was still
speaking…."

So it was Satan who took all this from Job and even this
could not drive Job away from God.

I have written in many previous notes that I have asked
God what His message is to me with these afflictions that I
have experienced over my years. I have never said to
anyone "Why me?" Instead I have asked "Why not me?"
 I'd like to consider myself a tough guy, stronger than many

and hardier to weather the turmoil brought upon me by these ailments. And sometimes maybe it helps to be stubborn too. And that I am. I think it has been better for me to have these torments than so many of my family and close friends. I know Jesus Christ has taken me in His arms to lead me forward. I have survived these times because I think God has this in His plan for me. He knows all and He knows I will tell others of His power, love and greatness. I know that day back in October last fall during the harvest when I could have gotten run over by the tractor it wasn't my own strength that kept my hand firmly on the rail to keep me from going under the rear tires of the tractor.

The Armor of God ~ Ephesians 6:10-18

Finally, be strong in the Lord and in his mighty power. Put on the full armor of God, so that you can take your stand against the devil's schemes. For our struggle is not against flesh and blood, but against the rulers, against the authorities, against the powers of this dark world and against the spiritual forces of evil in the heavenly realms. Therefore put on the full armor of God, so that when the day of evil comes, you may be able to stand your ground, and after you have done everything, to stand. Stand firm then, with the belt of truth buckled around your waist, with the breastplate of righteousness in place, and with your feet fitted with the readiness that comes from the gospel of peace. In addition to all this, take up the shield of faith, with which you can extinguish all the flaming arrows of the evil one. Take the helmet of salvation and the sword of the Spirit, which is the word of God. And pray in the Spirit on all occasions with all kinds of prayers and requests. With this in mind, be alert and always keep on praying for all the Lord's people.

Each day I put on the Armor of God and my feet are fitted with readiness. My mountain climbing boots that comes with knowing the Good Book and what it can do for me.

I have decided to "tag" some in this new post, not because I'm becoming conceited, not because I wish to have people read my Notes. I do this to tell others of God and His only Son. That I believe in His suffering for our sins. And maybe what I have written will help another know God in a better way. All prayers are answered. They might not be the answer we are looking for. The answers are what God knows is best for us. I prayed many times over the almost 3 years since the hit and run incident what it was supposed to mean. What is God's message to me?

If you declare with your mouth, "Jesus is Lord," and believe in your heart that God raised him from the dead, you will be saved. ~ Romans 10:9

* I want to add Pastor Kevin's side note to what I wrote about Paul. Kevin suggests that it might not be Paul's primary concern what people thought of him but rather that God was concerned that Paul would not become conceited. Paul, being human, had the same human nature as we ourselves do, prone to conceit. God was protecting him from that. ~~ I feel that Kevin's thought here might very well be correct and I thank Kevin for giving this perspective. +++

29

Forgive and free yourself from the evil one
March 6, 2013 at 5:07pm

Last Saturday I attended a Walk Through The Bible session on the New Testament at First Lutheran. It was a fun and interesting time for all of us who were there. One of the parting things the presenter wanted those of us who wished to do it anyway, was to write on the back of a card "Yes, with God's help I commit to read my Bible and pray for the next 30 days" and you signed the card and took it home with you.

I embarked on my quest to fulfill that commitment and I was amazed at how much clearer the reading of my Bible became after I made that decision to read and pray every day and not just when I felt like it. Some of the passages just about leapt out at me to poke me in the ribs to get my attention. Even verses that I have read many times before carried new meaning. A clarity that was so very profound I cannot explain it.

John 20:23 was one of the first:

(22) ...."Receive the Holy Spirit **(23) If you forgive anyone's sins, they are forgiven. If you do not forgive them, they are not forgiven."**

Another is 2 Corinthians 2:10-11 **(10)"When you forgive this man, I forgive him too. And when I forgive whatever needs to be forgiven, I do so with Christ's authority for your benefit (11) so that Satan will not outsmart us. For we are familiar with his evil schemes."**

Since the days I read these passages on Sunday and Monday I have thought many times about their true meaning. It was a bit hard to comprehend but as I had committed myself on Saturday it became clearer to me. I wrote "....with God's help...." and I feel this was a way for God to talk to me about something I couldn't let go of. I have had pictures of myself laying in the street after the hit and run driver had left me to die. I have looked at it many times over the many months since the incident. I also have pictures of the probable car, 16 of them to be exact. I had counted them. I know who the driver was and have been frustrated at the lack of forward movement by law enforcement to do something right. I have been upset at the laws and calousness of our society that this could happen. I have screamed in my mind at lawyers because they wouldn't listen to my pleas.

But God provided me help today because of that commitment I made last Saturday. I have really started enjoying an early Wednesday morning Bible study and while at the Bible study this morning it became very clear to me. I had left the house a bit earlier than I usually do because I was going to go to my office to get that folder with those 16 pictures and I was going to take them to my study group and proclaim my inability to forgive and ask them for their help in this self torture of mine. But when it was time to get out of my pickup and go inside for the study, I chickened out and left the folder in my locked pickup. The more we talked of things like forgiveness and the strength and power that God has given through our faith in Him, a revelation came upon me. Even though I was shaking and was quite apprehensive in what I knew I was about to do I also knew I had to take the bull by the horns and take control.

I told Pastor Kevin and the others I would be right back, that I had to get something out of my pickup. So I went outside and took a hold of my worn manila folder with the 16 photos and also the scissors that I had grabbed at the office earlier in the morning. I went and sat back down and Kevin could see the folder with the scissors laying on top and when the discussion had a bit of a lull Kevin asked what I wanted to do with what was sitting on the table in front of me.

I said it was confession time. I told the guys that in this folder were pictures of that incident and the car and that I knew who the driver was and that even though I have prayed to be able to forgive him, I had only prayed to myself and I felt I needed to confess to my peers that I needed to pray for forgiveness of this guy. To put myself humbly before God and ask for His forgiveness of this terrible thing that had such a steely grip on my soul. It is with humility at the foot of the Cross that I placed myself this morning and I was joined by the others who prayed with me and for me; asking for this man to be forgiven; to take this dark blemish from my heart.

When I got done praying it was as if a light was turned on. It was like the white elephant was lifted from my chest. Then we each took turns at clipping and snipping those pictures into shreds over the wastebasket.

I humbly ask God in the name of His only Son Jesus the Christ that I can continue to forgive those who have sinned against me and I ask for His strength and guidance that I will be able to live more Christ-like each day.

"Seek the LORD while he may be found; call upon him while he is near; let the wicked forsake his way, and the unrighteous man his thoughts; let him return to the LORD, that he may have compassion on him, and to our God, for he will abundantly pardon." ~ Isaiah 55:6-7

30

So, you want to judge another?
April 12, 2013 at 2:16pm

A couple weeks ago the red and pink equals sign as a profile picture was making the rounds on Facebook and it was upsetting to me to say the least. I finally had had enough and posted on my own status that I was "sickened" by it. I was chastised by some for this posting. I even lost at least a couple of "friends" over the post of mine. Some that are very close to me voiced their own displeasure over my status post. So I deleted the post from Facebook but not from my own mind. I was upset that others seemed to have opinions that I was supposed to accept and respect but my own was evidently deemed inconsequential so I was the one that was doing wrong.

I never let this episode leave my conscience though and with my day today being one that leaves some time to think this over some more, I did just that. I have made the statement, especially in the past few weeks, I believe that social issues such as alcoholism and drug addiction are human desires and choices. I have said that those who choose to have a sex change do so because of their human desire to choose this lifestyle. These things are not God-given in my opinion. They are truly human choices and if a person wants to have, say a sex change, I believe they are basically saying that "God made a mistake with me and I'm going to make it right."

I was chastised in that earlier post by a person who said that in their previous Sunday sermon at church part of the topic was "Judge not, lest ye be judged." This has spurned a desire in my own mind to find the truth. To read what the Bible says in judging. It has been a great afternoon as I have read, and I am now actually understanding better, what our scriptures say about judging those around us.

The verse above is Matthew 7:1 and now that I have read and think I understand it better I feel the verse that DIRECTLY follows that oft-quoted one needs to be addressed here. Matthew 7:2 "For in the same way you judge others, you will be judged, and with the measure you use, it will be measured to you." In the Old Testament you can read in Malachi 3:18" Then shall ye return, and discern between the righteous and the wicked, between him that serveth God and him that serveth not." It sure looks to me that we are actually supposed to be judging others. This judgment needs to be by the Law of God, but by judging others we need to be sure it is within His law. We can read in Proverbs 24:23 "These also are sayings of the wise: To show partiality in judging is not good." And in Isaiah 42:1 "Here is my servant, whom I uphold, my chosen one in whom I delight; I will put my Spirit on him, and he will bring justice to the nations" and Isaiah 42:19-21 "Who is blind but my servant, and deaf like the messenger I send? Who is blind like the one in covenant with me, blind like the servant of the Lord? You have seen many things, but you pay no attention; your ears are open, but you do not listen." It pleased the Lord for the sake of his righteousness to make his law great and glorious.

So if we do judge those around us we need to be correct in our scripture and we need to be respectful to those who we are addressing. As Psalms 37:30 advises us, we need to be wise in what we do and how we do it. "The mouths of the righteous utter wisdom, and their tongues speak what is just."

So in Matthew 7:1-7 Jesus was clearly addressing hypocrites—those who refuse to take responsibility for their own faults before judging the faults of others. We need to make sure our own house is in order before we judge others. Verse 6 talks about things that are sacred and not respected.

In John 7:24 Jesus is talking again when He says "Stop judging by mere appearances, and make a right judgment." Right there Jesus is telling us TO judge, but to make the right decision when we do. I hardly think He would have instructed us to judge if He didn't WANT us to judge.

The word judge in various forms such as judging, judgment, judgeth, etc., is in our Bible over 700 times. Maybe we need to use that word or words more often these days. Our generation is well described in Isaiah 59:8. "The way of peace they know not; and there is no judgment in their goings: they have made crooked paths: whosoever goeth therein shall not know peace." So our generation has refused to judge so now we have no peace? Wow....interesting and scary concept in my opinion.

A favorite writer and contributor to our Bible is the Apostle Paul. Paul wrote in 1 Corinthians 1:10"....be perfectly joined together in the same mind and in the same judgment."Would Paul have written this if judging really is wrong? Paul goes on to write in 1 Corinthians 2:15 "But he that is spiritual judgeth all things, yet he himself is judged of no man." I take from this verse that judging isn't a sin but in fact it is a characteristic of being a spiritual person. So is Satan hoping that we will NOT judge? That we rebuke each other when we do pass a judgment on our peers? So that we no longer please God when we do know His Law and will tell others of these Laws? Paul himself rebukes the Corinthians when they refused to follow the Law. Very clearly to me Paul writes that we need to judge people. We need to follow His Law first though or we will sin by being a hypocrite as Jesus told us.

Right and wrong should always be determined by God's word, not ours. King Solomon prayed to God to grant him wisdom in order to judge properly. James 1:5 says "If any of you lack wisdom, let him ask of God, that giveth to all men liberally, and upbraideth not; and it shall be given to him."

Lastly, we are not to forget to judge ourselves. Paul writes in 1 Corinthians 11:30-31 "For this cause many are weak and sickly among you, and many sleep. For if we judge ourselves, we should not be judged."

So in looking back at what prompted this writing of mine, did I make a mistake? Was I truly wrong in judging others? I don't like sitting on a fence but maybe the correct answer to my own question is yes AND no. Yes I was wrong in judging others the way I did and if anyone reading this felt wronged by my writing, please accept my apology in that. I should have been better informed of the Word of God about this testy subject. I need to respect others opinions as much as I demand my views to be respected. But I was right in a way because our scriptures do tell us that we can judge, if we do it in a proper way by the Law of God. And that's really the sticking point to me. Like I initially said toward the beginning of this letter is that these things I was addressing for the most part, homosexuality, gay marriage, alcoholism and drug addiction, are truly human desires and habits. They aren't God-given and with the sexual stuff I believe that those that choose these lifestyles are saying God made a mistake with me and I'm making a right out of a wrong.

1 Corinthians 5:12-13 says, "What business is it of mine to judge those outside the church? Are you not to judge those inside? God will judge those outside. Expel the wicked man from among you." So if do want to judge another, we need to have our own house in order and we need to adhere to our Biblical teachings. We will have to do this in accordance to the church and that church is Jesus the Christ.

"You have heard that it was said, 'Love your neighbor and hate your enemy.' But I tell you, love your enemies and pray for those who persecute you, that you may be children of your Father in heaven. He causes his sun to rise on the evil and the good, and sends rain on the righteous and the unrighteous. If you love those who love you, what reward will you get? Are not even the tax collectors doing that? And if you greet only your own people, what are you doing more than others? Do not even pagans do that? Be perfect, therefore, as your heavenly Father is perfect." ~~ Matthew 5:43-48 +++

I will pray to God that He will help me understand more and if I judge others that my own house will be in order so I cannot be deemed a hypocrite. To those who chastised me in person or in writing about my post a couple weeks ago, I say "Thank you for helping me understand better and to enrich my Faith to where I think it needs to be."

31

It's an Invisible War
July 25, 2013 at 10:53pm

The men's Wednesday morning Bible study group I enjoy being a part of has started studying "The Invisible War" by Chip Ingram. It is touted as "What every believer needs to know about Satan, demons and spiritual warfare." We just had one morning of about a 2 hour session but I am already very excited to learn more about this subject.

The national events of the past few weeks have captivated everyone's interest, even my own. The George Zimmerman trial for murder in the death of Trayvon Martin has made me open my mind more than I usually let it. And it will possibly surprise some by me saying this but it really has nothing to do with a racial overtone. It has nothing to do with the perception that Zimmerman is white which I have been told is not the truth if it even matters to anyone reading this note of mine. It isn't about Trayvon being a black. Or a militant like teen either. My own thoughts have been about the matter of this invisible war of spiritualism. I hadn't thought about why this trial had been bothering me until later that day after our first session on this study. When I was driving down the road my mind was wandering some as the traffic was non-existent for the most part so this debacle kept itself in the forefront of my mind.

The Narrow and Wide Gates

"Enter through the narrow gate. For wide is the gate and broad is the road that leads to destruction, and many enter through it. But small is the gate and narrow the road that leads to life, and only a few find it. ~ Matthew 7:13-14

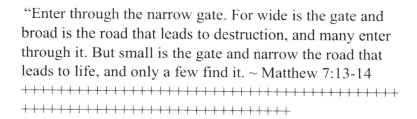

This passage is what I started thinking about when contemplating the Zimmerman trial aftermath. With so many rioting and protesting and others supporting Zimmerman and his claim of self-defense I was thinking and wondering are they all following the wide path? And not watching for the narrow gate? Is this just one more way for the devil to scheme against us and lead us away from God?

I have really questioned some things the past couple days because of this issue and the new study of ours. How many of the issues that we see and hear about today could be attributed to this invisible war? Whether it is in our own little personal lives dealing with jobs or family issues or larger like national or worldwide stuff?

A debate that doesn't seem to be winnable from any perspective is the marriage issue and the gay and lesbian rights and of course abortion. Is all this part of the devil's schemes to divide us? After all, it is this quote that we all should pay attention to:

United we stand, divided we fall

This quote is generally attributed to Aesop but John Dickinson used it in more recent times when our nation was contemplating independence from England in the late 1700s. But maybe it is a quote we should take to our faithful hearts and to reflect deeply on how we are being assaulted by the evil schemes in our lives.

Put on the full armor of God, so that you can take your stand against the devil's schemes. For our struggle is not against flesh and blood, but against the rulers, against the authorities, against the powers of this dark world and against the spiritual forces of evil in the heavenly realms. ~ Ephesians 6:11-12

For the secret power of lawlessness is already at work; but the one who now holds it back will continue to do so till he is taken out of the way. ~ 2 Thessalonians 2:7

See to it that no one takes you captive through hollow and deceptive philosophy, which depends on human tradition and the elemental spiritual forces of this world rather than on Christ. ~ Colossians 2:8

Since the children have flesh and blood, he too shared in their humanity so that by his death he might break the power of him who holds the power of death—that is, the devil— ~ Hebrews 2:14

Submit yourselves, then, to God. Resist the devil, and he will flee from you. ~ James 4:7

+++

We all probably think that our thoughts are really the way it is and should be. Whether politically, spiritually or morally. To me I seriously wonder if the battle against evil can be won if we continue to put ourselves and our ideals before those that God commanded for us.

Armor up +++

32

"Why are you here?"
September 30, 2013 at 1:07pm

What a wonderful month this September of 2013 has been
for me.

The early Wednesday morning Bible study sessions make
each week more enjoyable than the last one and I am
confident this will continue to progress in this way. But this
story really started in late August so I will begin there.

In the last part of August a fellow who had been attending
the Bible study earlier this year had returned after not being
able to attend because of work commitments. I will call
him PH. Then one Sunday after he had returned the
previous Wednesday he had to go in for a critical
emergency surgery. He almost died and probably would
have if he hadn't checked himself into the hospital. Then
the following Wednesday PH had called pastor Kevin about
5 that morning from his hospital bed. PH had torn all of his
IVs and other wires and hoses out of himself in the wee

hours of the morning and when the nurses had gotten into the room a short time after the alarms went off he had blood everywhere. PH had demons attacking him, not wanting to let go of him. You see, PH had moved here from another state some time ago and had a rough time of life in his previous home and he wanted to be in the presence of Christ. The dark side evidently had a grip on him and with him coming back to the Bible study they wanted him back. A spiritual battle rages inside him. On the one hand he wants to be with Christ and live for Him, but on the other hand his past haunts him and won't let go. Satan would rather see him dead than to surrender his life to Christ and that's the reason discouragement and depression took him to the point of despair,

and and wanting to take his own life. The more he seeks to find God, the more the enemy fights to keep him from doing so.

It might seem to us that whenever God is drawing anyone to Himself there is a real struggle. PH does want to be with Christ, but to some extent at least, he wants to hold on to certain things in his life that are sinful. This is a battle for his soul with warring forces waging the battle. I don't think that PH has been born again, which is why he is limited in his ability to overcome. When a person is truly "in Christ" God's grace gives him the ability to turn away from sin. But if a person is not born again, then change is more "religion" or man's efforts, than God's power at work within.

Kevin told us that PH was going to call his cell phone about the time we usually got the study session started so we could all pray with him and for him. This call was about 8-10 minutes in duration and when it concluded we pushed our regular session aside and discussed this affliction of PH's. Kevin brought up Philippians 1:1 where we read "Paul and Timothy, servants of Christ Jesus....." Some translations say "slaves" instead of "servants" and this was the core of my thoughts the next few hours. It was a great time talking about this as our session is "The Invisible War" by Chip Ingram. How fitting is this that in our study we get combat training with our own fellow soldiers of God?

Finally, be strong in the Lord and in his mighty power. Put on the full armor of God, so that you can take your stand against the devil's schemes. For our struggle is not against flesh and blood, but against the rulers, against the authorities, against the powers of this dark world and against the spiritual forces of evil in the heavenly realms. Therefore put on the full armor of God, so that when the day of evil comes, you may be able to stand your ground, and after you have done everything, to stand. Stand firm then, with the belt of truth buckled around your waist, with the breastplate

of righteousness in place, and with your feet fitted with the readiness that comes from the gospel of peace. In addition to all this, take up the shield of faith, with which you can extinguish all the flaming arrows of the evil one. Take the helmet of salvation and the sword of the Spirit, which is the word of God. And pray in the Spirit on all occasions with all kinds of prayers and requests. With this in mind, be alert and always keep on praying for all the Lord's people. ~ Ephesians 6:10-18
+++

When the session was over we talked of PH and what he had gone through. I left to go to work but this never was far from my mind. I had a slower day scheduled and after a couple calls to move those things to the next day I headed to Aberdeen to visit PH in the hospital. PH has no family close by and not a lot of friends yet and I know how it feels to be cooped up in a hospital all day long, days seemingly without end.

When I walked into the hospital room and PH and I had shared greetings he looked at me with an incredulous look and asked **"Why are you here?"** I reiterated that all of us in the study group were concerned about his well being and since my day was slow I wanted to drive to Aberdeen (an hour drive each way) to visit him, especially since he didn't have any family close by to come see him. We went over that morning's Bible discussion and I read Kevin's

Facebook post about Philippians 1:1. He thanked me but then asked again, **"But why are you here?"**

I decided to tell him more. This is what I shared with PH:

I have had an interesting and Blessed life that God has granted me. I was run over by a farm tractor before I was age 6. I was in the hospital for 6 weeks and then on bed rest at home for another 6 weeks. I had 3 heart attacks in 17 days in 1999 at age 39. I was hit by a car in a hit and run incident in November of 2009 and left for dead when the driver drove away. I am dealing with Leukemia today. I am here with you today because Christ wants me here. If I want to be a servant of Christ, a slave of Christ, I NEED to be here today with you PH. I am here on this earth today because Christ wants me here.

We prayed together for a few minutes after this exchange and after some small talk I went back home.

Now I fast forward to this past week. A guy who is quite close to my wife and I is going through a difficult time of his own and I took the time to go to his place a few states away to visit and talk to him. It was a great time tagging along with him while he performed his daily duties and we had some awesome skull sessions at night trying to work our way through this ordeal of his. I related the hospital story to him and I told him the same thing as I did PH. I am here because Christ wants me here. I felt very honored when I saw tears coming down his cheeks when he realized that might be true. That Christ wanted me there because Christ wants him closer to the Word.

It was an absolute joyous 12 hour drive back home. In those darkest days when I was still in full recovery mode from the hit and run, I asked, I pleaded, I prayed to God what He wanted me to do with this new life. I knew there had to be a message for me in all these afflictions I have endured.

A Time for Everything

There is a time for everything,
   and a season for every activity under the heavens:
   a time to be born and a time to die,
   a time to plant and a time to uproot,
   a time to kill and a time to heal,
   a time to tear down and a time to build,
   a time to weep and a time to laugh,
   a time to mourn and a time to dance,
   a time to scatter stones and a time to gather them,
   a time to embrace and a time to refrain from
embracing,
   a time to search and a time to give up,
   a time to keep and a time to throw away,

a time to tear and a time to mend,
a time to be silent and a time to speak,
a time to love and a time to hate,
a time for war and a time for peace.

What do workers gain from their toil? I have seen the burden God has laid on the human race. He has made everything beautiful in its time. He has also set eternity in the human heart; yet no one can fathom what God has done from beginning to end. I know that there is nothing better for people than to be happy and to do good while they live. That each of them may eat and drink, and find satisfaction in all their toil—this is the gift of God. I know that everything God does will endure forever; nothing can be added to it and nothing taken from it. God does it so that people will fear him. ~ Ecc 3:1-14 +++

We all are here because Christ wants us here. Maybe it's important for us to ask ourselves that question PH asked me, before we ALL are wondering and asking God why things happen the way they do. We all have a spiritual battle raging around us if we are keen and able to recognize them. They might be very real like they are for PH or they might be more subtle such as in our agonizing over family issues, financial concerns, job uncertainties. These are all signs that I feel are very real and prayer is an answer for us, especially if we can reinforce our army with other soldiers wearing the Armor of God. Peace and blessings to all. +++

Why are you here?

"Let me tell you why you are here. You're here to be salt-seasoning that brings out the God-flavors of this earth. If you lose your saltiness, how will people taste godliness? You've lost your usefulness and will end up in the garbage. "Here's another way to put it: You're here to be light, bringing out the God-colors in the world. God is not a secret to be kept. We're going public with this, as public as a city on a hill. If I make you light-bearers, you don't think I'm going to hide you under a bucket, do you? I'm putting you on a light stand. Now that I've put you there on a hilltop, on a light stand - shine! Keep open house; be generous with your lives. By opening up to others, you'll prompt people to open up with God, this generous Father in heaven. ~ Matthew 5: 13-16 +++

David Christenson
September 6

There are probably just a few things that I'm pretty sure of, that I will admit. I'm sure this will be a difficult day for me because we will bury a good friend of mine. I'm sure it will also be a difficult day for his family and all of his many friends. I'm sure he is in a better place now and his body is no longer wracked with those terrible afflictions.

I had known Gary Zuehlke for many years prior to my days as a salesman at the local John Deere store. Gary came in about mid-morning pretty much every day after feeding the cattle and other chores to get a Diet Coke and to check up on the many things that were happening around the store and around the community. You see, Gary was very community oriented and it was one of the important things in his life. His family was always first and foremost and he was so very proud of his family the whole time I ever knew him. His community was also very high on his list of important things in his earthly life. A few years ago when Britton was to celebrate it's 125th anniversary Gary was part of the group of people lining things up. I had intentions of just going along with the flow and enjoying things as they happened. By this time I had left John Deere and had an office on the corner of the main 4-way stop in town. Just a block from where most of the celebration festivities were to be held. Gary stopped into my office many times to make sure I was working I suppose but to have a Diet Coke and when he was doing treatment and therapy it was for a bottle of water. But one day when the planning for the celebration was in full swing Gary stopped in again and over his Diet Coke he asked if I would be able to help with setting up the tents, help with getting his Uffda Brudders singing group's stuff around for their performance and just help in general. I could never say no to Gary. He was always so sincere in his quest to help and recruit others into his fold. And I will tell you, those days of helping with the celebration are moments that I smile about when reflecting upon them.

The times I went out to the farm to visit the past month or so were hard because I could see that he wasn't going to be with us much longer. But I relish those moments and hopefully always will. Yesterday was also a hard day when my wife and I went to be with the family at the funeral home. Then later in the evening I was at the toy shop at the farm with the family and friends as they gathered after the service. We all traded Gary stories. We all cried. But we all reflected on the positive influence our husband, father, grandfather, friend and business partner had over us.

Good-bye Gary Zuehlke. I am so very proud and glad that I have known you and that you considered me a friend. You were one of the best of friends a person could ever wish for.

Why I wrote this

When I was hospitalized in Fargo my doctors didn't want me to have access to my cell phone nor did they want me to have my laptop computer available either. I was told they reasoned that brain injury patients sometimes have issues with these communication tools and some have trouble adjusting to their new condition. Early on, nobody really knew how injured my brain was and to what extent I could recover. But after about two weeks in the hospital the doctors were of the opinion that my brain injury wasn't to the level that these things would be likely to happen so I was allowed to use these electronic tools.

I was very pleased to log into my email account and also Facebook. It was fun to be able to text people and to actually call out and to receive calls.

The doctors had initially told my family that I would be lucky to be home for Christmas which was over five weeks after the injury. I wasn't aware of that prognosis until after I was released.

I knew I was hurt and I knew it was a tough situation. But I could not use a reset button. It was water under the bridge so I was left with the present and the future. I have thought for a long time that attitude and effort are a couple of things we have some control over so when I started to regain some cognizance I decided I would do my best to have a good attitude and apply a good effort at the therapies I was to under-go while still in the hospital. So I embarked on that strategy when the therapeutic sessions started in late November.

With that attitude thought process I also decided to start recording things I was dealing with and experiencing via my Facebook page. I knew that so many people had been talking and asking my family about me and how things were going so in part I thought maybe this would alleviate some of the pressure the family had in this regard by having my friends and relatives read my own posts and give them an opportunity to ask me the questions they were wanting an answer to. A reader will find numerous spelling and grammatical mistakes and other related issues in this manuscript of mine. I have left them here for a purpose. Many that know me well have seen where I have a few pet peeves and some of those are spelling and grammar. I decided to leave those mistakes in this writing to demonstrate how I was affected with those head and brain injuries. I was probably functioning somewhere in the range of a 4th, 5th or 6th grade mentality when I left the hospital and it has taken time to try to redevelop those skills I possessed prior to the injuries. I still struggle with these things although not as much. It has not been uncommon for me to have to think about things more than I used to and in some cases when I can't word things the way

I want because of not being able to remember properly I just opt for a simpler and easier wording.

In all this, I started questioning how durable and strong my faith was and maybe this is evident in my early writings in this manuscript. My faith has grown plenty in the years since the incident. It is my hope that the reader can also see this growth and can gain some faithful strength of their own because of these writings of mine.

Thank you for being here for me. I know why you are here.

+++

David Christenson
January 18, 2010

Please put this as your status if you know someone who is a Mob Wars/Mafia Wars addict as we are trying to raise awareness.~ MW addiction affects the lives of many. There is still no known cure for MW addiction but you can raise awareness. 93% won't copy and paste this, because they are too busy playing MW...excuse me I am about to level up....

David Christenson
January 20, 2010

If you are a parent with the greatest kids on earth then copy and repost this and let's give our kids the recognition they need! I love my kids. They may not be perfect, but none of us are... I LOVE THEM UNCONDITIONALLY!!!

David Christenson
January 21, 2010

attended the calf sale today. Was simply awesome to be out and about the town and to visit with all the guys that I was always with at this type of business. Felt really good to have so many come up to me and shake my hand and tell me it was good to see me and that I was able and interested in going out on the town.

David Christenson

January 27, 2010

Spending today at my office trying to get stuff sorted, etc. First time I have been in here since before the accident. Was really a great sense of feeling to once again be here and to use my desk phone to call people with once again. Tomorrow is the ortho doc to see when I can once again drive.....

David Christenson

January 28, 2010

When I stand before God at the end of my life, I would hope that I would not have a single bit of talent left, and could say, "I used everything you gave me." ~Erma Bombeck

David Christenson

January 28, 2010

Know that sometimes the writing material you have is your own blood. -- Daniel Berrigan

David Christenson

January 28, 2010 via mobile

Good appt at ortho doc today. Can put full body weight on leg. Also probably attend driving school in 2 weeks. Another step in right direction for me.

David Christenson
January 29, 2010

Walked without the aid of my walker today. Leg got tired from so much non-use (2 1/2 months now) but still felt very good to actually make the leg do the work again. Everyday something shows it's improvement from the previous day.

David Christenson
February 1, 2010 via mobile

You should always give 100% at work...12% Monday; 23% Tuesday; 40% Wednesday; 20% Thursday; 5% Friday.

David Christenson
February 5, 2010

Just got home from Fargo where my IVC filter was removed. There was a blood clot in the filter so the filter did it's job while it was implanted. Just one more step in the right direction for me so has been another good day.

David Christenson
February 9, 2010

Another good doctor appointment today. I am now able to go without the Aspen collar around my neck at all anymore and will be able to start the process to get back to driving my Sierra GMC 4-door pickup as early as next week. SWEET !!!!

David Christenson
February 10, 2010

Just got back to my office after walking to the post office to get my mail. First time I have ventured out "on my own" since I started my recovery. It used to take less than 10 minutes when I have walked this in the past and took the better part of 20 minutes today. But it was progress and that is what I am aiming for each and every day.

David Christenson
February 10, 2010

I like beating the oddsmakers. In reading the reports from the doctors about my accident I have learned that my Glasgow Coma Scale was "3-5" depending upon which department was reporting. A low score (as 3 to 5) indicates a poor chance of recovery and for a high score (as 8 to 15) indicates a good chance of recovery. Hmmm.....

David Christenson
February 20, 2010 via mobile

"Whatever you do, do it with all your might. Work at it, early and late, in season and out of season." -PT Barnum

David Christenson
February 20, 2010

Sitting in my office today and enjoying life. I was able to drive myself from home to my usual parking place for my white 2008 GMC 4-door Sierra. This was my first unsupervised drive since 14 November, 2009 when I was smucked by the hit and run driver while I was walking home that night. Life is good.....

David Christenson

February 22, 2010

Today is the first time in about 100 days that both Gretchen and I drove to work at the same time. This is possible because I am a licensed driver once again after my TBI has healed enough to allow me to drive again. Going to be a good day...

David Christenson

February 28, 2010

"God places the heaviest burden on those who can carry it's weight." ~ Reggie White, NFL Hall of Famer

David Christenson

March 15, 2010

Good-bye Buss. You blazed a good trail for those of us who follow in your steps. For over 99 years you set an example that many of us could only look up to. And left us many stories that we could learn from and laugh at. Buss Tisher, 19 August 1910 - 15 March 2010. Thank you for the lesson of life. You rode the good ride.....

David Christenson

April 8, 2010

Football isn't necessarily won by the best players. It's won by the team with the best attitude. ~~ George Allen

David Christenson

April 9, 2010

A true love story was lived my Buss and Anje Tisher. They were married for 76 years before Buss passed away 25 days ago. Anje left us to rejoin Buss this afternoon. My only regret is that I didn't know you long enough Anje. Thank you for being a part of my life.

David Christenson

April 26, 2010

RIP Wally Steiner 4/1/1955 - 4/26/2010. Hope you can throw the fastball for strikes in your next start. Enjoyed playing the world's greatest game with you as your left fielder.

David Christenson

April 26, 2010

If I could make the diving catch for you one more time Wally .... I would do my best. I always knew you as a lefty would demand an extreme effort by your left fielder. RIP my friend ....

David Christenson

May 2, 2010 via mobile

It's hard to make a comeback when you haven't been anywhere.

David Christenson

May 9, 2010

I told my neuropsychologist I feel like I am in a wheel barrow. She told me not to let people push me around ....

David Christenson
May 11, 2010

When you were born, you cried and the world rejoiced. Live your life so that when you die,the world cries and you rejoice.

David Christenson
May 26, 2010

If you do a good job for others, you heal yourself at the same time, because a dose of joy is a spiritual cure. ~ Dietrich Bonhoeffer

David Christenson
June 20, 2010

It doesn't take much to be a good father. A big heart to love your kids no matter what. Big arms to hold them and carry them when they can't carry themselves. And a strong back to carry the family through the storms and the calm. I am glad to wear the Dad badge! I wouldn't want to be anything else.

David Christenson
July 18, 2010

Life is a great big canvas and you should throw all the paint on it you can. ~ Danny Kaye

David Christenson
August 14, 2010

is wondering why kamikaze pilots wore helmets....

David Christenson
September 2, 2010

There is no sudden entrance into Heaven. Slow is the ascent by the path of Love. ~ Ella Wheeler Wilcox

David Christenson
September 7, 2010

Today's goal: Together with Josh Kraft and Randy Damgaard I will be meeting with the county commissioners at 10:30 to discuss a new facility for our great EMT crew here in Britton. We have been talking with many in the area about this and it seems to have financial backing so should help the commission in that regard.

David Christenson
September 14, 2010

10 months.... some might say it goes too quickly. The last 10 months have literally been a lifetime for me and my family. These last 10 months have been very long while also being quite short. I know that sounds strange but sometimes the truth is a strange thing to hold. Goodnight everyone. Make sure your loved ones know how you feel about them. You might not get the chance to do so again.

David Christenson
September 30, 2010

Great day today. Harvesting soybeans at the farm and I hauled beans to Oakes. More of this tomorrow. Sometimes we miss the things we can't do anymore, especially when those things are taken away from us. It's been almost 11 months since we were given that stark reminder. It was a VERY gratifying feeling to do this and to spend time with my family after that dark day last November.

David Christenson

October 8, 2010 via mobile

Plenty of people miss their share of happiness because they didn't stop to enjoy it. - William Feather

David Christenson

October 12, 2010

Some people, myself included, hold their Faith close, maybe even in their pocket each day. But I admire those like my friend Dennis B. because he chose long ago to wear his Faith on his sleeve for all to see and in the hope that others will learn of the Word.

Dennis Barnhill posted to**David Christenson**

October 12, 2010

"For I know the plans I have for you," declares the LORD, "plans to prosper you and not to harm you, plans to give you hope and a future."- Jeremiah 29:11

David Christenson

October 14, 2010 via mobile

11 months .... A lifetime ago ...

David Christenson

October 14, 2010

For I am not ashamed of the gospel: for it is the power of God unto salvation to every one that believeth; to the Jew first, and also to the Greek. ~ Romans 1:16

David Christenson
October 22, 2010 via mobile

How can there be a limited lifetime warranty?

David Christenson
October 23, 2010

Great day today. The harvest at the farm is done. Terrific feeling to be a part of the harvest through the whole year after having much of it stolen from us last year by that unknown driver last November 14th. Such an awesome experience that is hard to put into words so this will have to do for now.

David Christenson
October 30, 2010

Tonight it will be 50 weeks since I was smucked by the hit and run driver. Sometimes toughness can be more than muscle and brawn. Sometimes Faith will be the strength a person needs in those difficult times that come their way.

David Christenson
November 6, 2010 via mobile

51 weeks ... 358 days .... A lifetime ago in many ways. I am blessed with great family & friends to help keep sanity after a cruel moment in time.

David Christenson
November 11, 2010

Sunday, 14 November, is the 'anniversary' of the crime that caused injuries to me and my family. The perpetrator has not been caught/charged as yet. They stole security and peace from my family but they did not, and cannot steal who we are, the Faith that holds us and that we hold close to us.

David Christenson
November 11, 2010

I am a hero who never fails, I can't be bothered with such details. ~ Underdog

David Christenson
November 11, 2010

With but few exceptions, it is always the underdog who wins through sheer willpower. ~ Johnny Weissmuller

David Christenson
November 11, 2010

I never expect to lose. Even when I'm the underdog, I still prepare a victory speech. ~ H. Jackson Brown, Jr.

David Christenson
November 11, 2010

Don't talk to me about aesthetics or tradition. Talk to me about what sells and what's good right now. And what the American people like is to think the underdog still has a chance. ~ George Steinbrenner

David Christenson
November 11, 2010

If you're an underdog, mentally disabled, physically disabled, if you don't fit in, if you're not as pretty as the others, you can still be a hero. ~ Steve Guttenberg

David Christenson
November 19, 2010

Reconnecting time today. Went to Fargo and met up with many of the nurses and therapists who were instrumental in helping me with my recovery. Joy, Brad, Tracy and Pam were just a few of those that were helping me and my family when help was really needed. I left messages for Heather and Nadine as they were either off today or at the North campus

David Christenson
November 22, 2010

Just got the call that I will need to be at the surgical center tomorrow a.m. to get my shoulder worked on. It is time to move forward.

David Christenson
November 26, 2010 via mobile

I'm wondering if a book about failure doesn't sell, is it a success?

From one man he made every nation of men,
that they should inhabit the whole earth;
and he determined the *times set for them*
and the *exact places where they should live*.
God did this so that men would seek him and
perhaps reach out for him and find him,
though he is not far from each of us.
Acts 17:26-27

In *Why Are You Here?*, we see the story of events and circumstances that have shaped the life of it's author. Besides the events, there are relationships and faith systems, emotions and convictions which all played a part in bringing David Christenson to this place in his life. More than that, there is a God who directed the course of these things, and did so for a specific reason: that Dave might know God.

I came to know Dave through what some might call coincidence…through Facebook of all things. A mutual friend had come to know Christ and expressed his faith through postings on Facebook, only to be mocked by certain "friends" as a "Bible thumper." Dave and I encouraged Josh in his faith, and soon the three of us began meeting weekly as friends who read the Bible together and ask questions about life and this God who is the source of life. That "coincidence" was yet another example of how God involves himself in our lives bringing about his purposes. That "coincidence" is really a blessing sent from God.

May the reading of this book help you recognize the many things God has done in your own story, so that you would "seek him, and perhaps reach out for him and find him," for he is not far from you. ~ Pastor Kevin Koop -- Cornerstone Bible Church Britton, SD

3 crosses, one for you, one for me, one for all of us.